Praise for

Saturdays with Stella

"As a dog lover and the owner of a 'precarious puppy' named Jake, I fell in love with *Saturdays with Stella*. I adored the way Allison Pittman took me into her relationship with an insecure dog, reminding me of the importance of accepting God's love for just who I am. I'm already thinking of a dozen people who will love this book, and I can't wait to share it!"

— TRICIA GOYER, author of fifteen books, including
Generation NeXt Marriage

"Spend a Saturday with Stella, and you'll have a new friend for life, along with an amazing perspective on what it means to walk with God."

— SIGMUND BROUWER, author of *Broken Angel* and
Who Made the Moon?

"If only we could all be like Stella—sitting, staying, and coming when our Master calls. Not that Stella is perfect, but though she sometimes regresses (backslides), disobeys (rebels), and wallows in the garbage (don't we all?), she knows her master and always returns repentant and grateful for grace. Imagine that: a dog for a role model!"

— TAMARA LEIGH, author of *Splitting Harriet* and
Faking Grace

"Humorous examples of Stella's misconduct and learning lace the pages of Allison Pittman's book, and each one parallels our relationship with the Heavenly Master. Commands from an Intermediate Obedience canine class filter into scriptural charges whispered by a loving Father. Allison Pittman has woven a funny, touching, inspirational book. A must-read for those who long to walk with God and not strain at the leash."

—EILEEN KEY, author of *Dog Gone!*

"Pittman has dug up a backyard treasure in *Saturdays with Stella*. Her wit, wisdom, and wagging-of-tales will cause you to laugh, sigh, and *sit up* in anticipation of the next chapter. Stella captures your heart like Pittman captures God's truth. She reveals the essence of our need for spiritual obedience yet serves it in a way that makes us beg for more. I highly recommend you reserve a spot for this must read."

—LINDA GOLDFARB, founder of Triune-Living
Ministries, national speaker, syndicated radio talk
show host, and columnist

"*Saturdays with Stella* is a delightful book for dog lovers. Allison Pittman uses the commands that she teaches her dog at obedience school to teach us how to 'sit' and 'wait' on the Lord. And although we may fail, just as Stella did at obedience school, God's love and grace are sufficient for us all."

—SUSAN OSBORN, director of the Christian Commu-
nicator Manuscript Critique Service and author of
29 books

Saturdays with Stella

How My Dog Taught Me to Sit, Stay, and Come When God Calls

Allison Pittman

MULTNOMAH
BOOKS

SATURDAYS WITH STELLA
PUBLISHED BY MULTNOMAH BOOKS
12265 Oracle Boulevard, Suite 200
Colorado Springs, Colorado 80921
A division of Random House Inc.

Scripture quotations are taken from the Holy Bible, New International Version®. NIV®. Copyright © 1973, 1978, 1984 by International Bible Society. Used by permission of Zondervan Publishing House. All rights reserved.

Italics in Scripture quotations reflect the author's added emphasis.

Details in some anecdotes and stories have been changed to protect the identities of the persons or dogs involved.

ISBN 978-1-60142-139-5

Published in association with William K. Jensen Literary Agency.

Published in the United States by WaterBrook Multnomah, an imprint of The Doubleday Publishing Group, a division of Random House Inc., New York.

MULTNOMAH is a trademark of Multnomah Books, and is registered in the U.S. Patent and Trademark Office. The colophon is a trademark of Multnomah Books.

Library of Congress Cataloging-in-Publication Data
Pittman, Allison.
     Saturdays with Stella : how my dog taught me to sit, stay, and come when God calls / Allison Pittman.
         p. cm.
     ISBN 978-1-60142-139-5
     1. Dog owners—Religious life. 2. Dogs—Religious aspects—Christianity. 3. Pets—Religious aspects—Christianity. 4. Animals—Religious aspects—Christianity. I. Title.
     BV4596.A54P57 2008
     277.3'082092—dc22
     [B]
                                                                                         2008020246

Printed in the United States of America
2009

10 9 8 7 6 5 4 3 2

For Mikey,
who finds a way to be master of the house
while letting me be Queen.

And my boys
Ryan, Jack, and Charlie,
who deserve an echoing chorus of, "Good boy!"

Finally, thank you, Katie,
for putting Stella's life in my hands.
May God richly bless you as you seek to walk with Him.

Contents

Acknowledgments ix

Introduction: *"Divine Puppy Drop"* .1

1 Quiet Time, Belly Up: *"Settle."* 11

2 At the Master's Feet: *"Sit!"* 23

3 The Best-Laid Plans: *"Down!"* 35

4 A Bird in the Mouth: *"Drop It!"* 47

5 Yours, Mine, and…Well, Mine: *"Leave It!"* 59

6 Everything's Better with Cheddar: *"Take It!"* 75

7 Cats and Frogs and Big, Barky Dogs: *"Let's Go!"* 85

8 Praise for the Invisible Dog: *"Come!"* 99

9 Patience Is Averting: *"Wait!"* 113

10 A Hefty Promise: *"Watch Me!"* 127

11 Clean Up, Aisle Seven: *"Stay!"* 145

Author's Note 163

Acknowledgments

First of all, I give thanks to my Lord and Savior Jesus Christ, who brought Stella into my life so I could experience just a taste of His infinite love for me.

Thank you, Lisa Pittman, for your awesome photography skills. I've always said that Stella reminds me of Audrey Hepburn, and you did such a great job of capturing her beauty. You truly have an eye for the soul, my sister!

Thank you, Alice and Brian and everybody at Multnomah, for seeing this story long before it was a single word on a page.

Thank you, Bill Jensen—Alpha Agent!—for being so strong and so smart and so supportive. May you always find peace on your two-mile loop.

Finally, thank you, Jean Pittman. I'm blessed to have your son as both my husband and best friend. You were the most intuitive person I've ever met, and Stella absolutely loved you. Thank you for being so generous with your life on this earth, and I cannot wait to see you in the new one!

For this reason I kneel before the Father, from whom his whole family in heaven and on earth derives its name. I pray that out of his glorious riches he may strengthen you with power through his Spirit in your inner being, so that Christ may dwell in your hearts through faith. And I pray that you, being rooted and established in love, may have power, together with all the saints, to grasp how wide and long and high and deep is the love of Christ, and to know this love that surpasses knowledge—that you may be filled to the measure of all the fullness of God.

EPHESIANS 3:14–19

Introduction

"Divine Puppy Drop"

*B*efore Stella, there was Neumann, and Neumann was perfect. In all of his eleven years, he never chewed a shoe, never woke the neighbors with his barking, never pounced on anyone from across the room. Neumann knew how to be at my feet without being under them; he knew his place on the bed was at the foot, not the pillow. Living with Neumann was less like having a dog and more like sharing a home with a gentlemanly old uncle who insists on wearing his suit coat and tie even though he hasn't been gainfully employed for at least twenty years. He came into rooms and onto couches only when expressly invited and vacated them with the slightest gesture. His greatest fault was that he suffered malodorous problems when he ate spicy foods.

Neumann was *my* dog. I couldn't take more than three steps without him right at my side—silent and unassuming.

My husband, Mike, and I hadn't been looking for a dog at all; he simply showed up on our doorstep—fully grown, ate a piece of cheese, and never left. When Neumann was young, he could jump so high, a specific command would bring his front paws to my shoulders. When I was pregnant with my twin sons, I was terrified that he might jump up as I held one of the babies, so I dressed a teddy bear in a onesie I'd received as a shower gift, held it in my arms, and told Neumann, "Don't jump!"

He never jumped to my shoulders again.

Neumann, with his penchant for short walks and long naps, was the ideal dog for me, but he wasn't really a fun family dog. He wasn't about to chase a Frisbee or wear a bandanna. As they grew up, my sons longed for some sort of beautiful romping dog—a golden retriever, a lab, a German shepherd—anything that could run across a field with its fur billowing in slow motion. They begged for a new puppy.

"No way," I'd tell them. "Neumann could never adjust to life with another dog. It wouldn't be fair to him."

"Maybe we could get another dog as soon as Neumann 'goes away,'" they'd say, curling their little fingers in the requisite quotation marks.

"Listen," I told them, "I've had Neumann a lot longer than I've had you, and you'd just better hope the house doesn't ever burn down so I won't have to choose which one I'd save."

As it turned out, Neumann did "go away" long before he actually died. Toxins released from his aging, diseased liver induced a kind of canine dementia, and for the last year of his life, he roamed the house unaware of his surroundings, to the extent of not even knowing if he was in the living room or out in the yard. He stopped making eye contact, and the unnerving way that he stared past me broke my heart. Our vet confirmed that he was in quite a bit of gastric pain, and the stiff movement of his joints served as further evidence of his constant suffering. Just before the Thanksgiving holiday during his eleventh year as part of our family, Neumann was allowed to find quiet peace.

And I fell apart. For months afterward, I would come home from work, open the door to my empty house and say, "Hey, Neumy-neum!" just as I had for over a decade. Not *every* day, of course, like I did when he was alive, but on those really good days when I was full of fun stories and happy to be home to share them.

After a suitable period of mourning, my sons came up with the same old questions. Could we get a new dog? I reminded them that Neumann was so special because *he* had come to *us*. I said that if God wanted us to have a new dog, He would drop one right in our yard.

"Just be patient," I told them, "and pray."

Meanwhile, I was praying too. Something about wanting a canine hedge of protection.

A year passed, and while visiting my in-laws at Christmastime, my niece walked in with a tiny, shiny puppy of indefinable breed(s). Onyx black, save for an ermine-like breast and a freshly docked tail, the pup had been abandoned in an apartment complex parking lot. Searches and posters had failed to produce an owner, and a shelter loomed if the little thing didn't find a home.

> *If God wanted us to have a new dog, He would drop one right in our yard.*

I took the puppy in my hand and held her, nose to nose, up to my face. She had a single star of white fur in the middle of her forehead.

"I'm going to name her Stella," I said.

So the boys had an answer to their prayer, just as I'd hoped they would. With a divine puppy drop straight into our family. One would think that the result would be a wash of great joy. And I guess it was, in a James 1:2 kind of way—you know, all the joy that's supposed to come in the midst of trials—because it seemed straightaway that our enjoyment of Stella would be a test of faith and a development of perseverance.

She wasn't a bad dog—no worse than any puppy, I assume. Yes, she chewed things, and yes, she dug holes, and yes, she yapped incessantly at times, and finally, yes, she was prone to piddle on the floor. It was this last bit of misbehavior that threatened to rip our family to pieces.

We did everything right in housebreaking Stella, and by "we" I include all members of my family and Stella herself. We were consistent. We offered rewards and praise; Stella accepted them. She scratched on the door; we opened it. We opened the door; she ran out. With all matters of urinary business successfully settled in the yard, it

> *While visiting my in-laws at Christmastime, my niece walked in with a tiny, shiny puppy of indefinable breed(s).*

seemed the constant carpet-prone indiscretions had little to do with any pressing potty need. A checkup with our veterinarian diagnosed the problem: submissive urination.

Apparently there are two extremes when it comes to canine behavior: dangerous aggression and overt submission. Most dogs—the easiest dogs—find their place in the family pack somewhere in the middle, recognizing the authority of the master of the house while feeling secure enough in their position to protect it when necessary. In a pack, urinating is a sign of submission, and Stella was suffering from a debilitating case of insecurity. She was constantly trying to reassure us of her loyalty, desperately trying to please us with her acquiescence, and we were ever the more frustrated because of it.

When she went to the door to go outside, we would praise her for her initiative, and she would urinate—just a little—before running through the door. When she came in after doing her bit, we would congratulate the effort, and she would release just a tad more in recognition of our praise.

Then followed a muddled, hollering mass of confusion as the same mouths that had offered such praise now brought forth ugly sounds of rebuke. Stella would look up at us, her brown eyes pleading, *What do you people want from me?* Because, bless her heart, she was trying. After all, if we told her to get off the couch, she would "submit" immediately, then hop down. Same if she was on our bed. Whenever we walked through the front door, she would "submit" in greeting—right there in the hardwood entryway. If we had an armful of groceries, we might just slip on her "submission," as we did in the kitchen when she expressed her gratitude for any tasty treat.

Our vet told us the solution was to have complete and utter tranquility in the household to avoid aggravating her already nervous nature. We were instructed never to look her in the eye and never to speak to her in anything but a calm, soothing voice. She should never be praised in a high-pitched

tone and never be reprimanded with anything but an unruf-
fled, half whispered, "No." For a time, any casual observer
would think that every member of our household was under
the influence of heavy medication as we slowly maneuvered
through the rooms, inviting Stella to go outside, come inside,
and, "Please, if you wouldn't mind terribly, drop that slipper.
Thank you so much." We all spoke as if auditioning to be the
voice of OnStar, and it worked.

For a while.

But then, in a moment of weakness, overcome by the il-
logical love I had for this dog, I hunkered down, looked Stella
straight in the eye, and told her she was such a good, pretty
girl. Simultaneously, my husband viewed the scene and, like
something from a cheesy action film, yelled, "Stoooooop!"

Torn between appreciation for my praise and apology for
my husband's anger, Stella ping-ponged between the two of
us, leaving a little trail of submission on the formerly beige
Berber carpet. I spent the rest of the day trying to force the
vein back under the skin of my husband's neck. I never knew
you could actually hear the sound of a heart hardening.

Stella was on shaky ground, and it was up to me to defend her.

"Don't you see?" I pleaded, seeing her through the eyes of
grace. "She's actually giving us a gift!"

But Mike only saw her through eyes bulged out by the rising blood pressure behind them. "We can't live like this."

Deep down I knew he was right.

The answer came days later when, without any conscious plan to do so, I walked into our local pet store and saw the sign that would change our lives.

Obedience Classes

Puppies

Potty Training

Intermediate (for dogs six months old or older)

Six Weeks

$99

There was one slot left in the Intermediate Obedience class that would meet for the first time the following Saturday, and I didn't think twice about signing up. After all, I loved Stella with all my heart, and even though our finances were shaky at best, no sacrifice seemed too great. I wrote out the check, already excited about the changes that would come about, envisioning our new life together as she would learn to come to me, to walk with me, to follow me.

And yet, by the time the six Saturdays were through, it was I who learned what it meant to truly follow *my* Master.

1

Quiet Time, Belly Up

"Settle."

He will quiet you with his love.

ZEPHANIAH 3:17

The class is set up in the back of the pet store—a circle of chairs cordoned off by a collection of baby gates. We're almost late because Stella, ever fearful of the unknown, had to stop, cower, and tinkle a few drops at every aisle. I look wistfully at the other dogs—the ones not there for Intermediate Obedience. They bound at their owners' feet, heads up and alert, tongues lolling with pure canine joy as they take in all the smells and sounds of their foray into the world of human retail.

Not Stella.

Stella's view of the store consists of one shiny, white concrete square after another, sliding in smooth succession under her nose as she is dragged, lock-legged and head down, to the plastic octagonal classroom. She really doesn't want to go in there. When we get to the open gate, she hunkers down, whines, and back-pedals her paws like something from a cartoon.

"C'mon, Stella bella!" I say, plastering on a smile that I hope will compensate for this dysfunctional display. After a few more tugs, we're in.

It's like the first day of any class. The instructor, Ramon, goes around the circle giving each of us the opportunity to introduce ourselves, our dogs, and the dilemmas that brought us to Intermediate Obedience. Since we're the last in the circle, we'll be the last ones to speak, which is fine with me. It gives me a chance to survey Stella's classmates, whose following names and breeds have been changed to protect the not-so-innocent.

First we meet Prima and Donna, a pair of Yorkshire terriers whose unrestrained barking at the car's windshield wipers makes driving hazardous for their middle-aged owners. Then there's Blanca, a three-month-old yellow lab whose behavior problems are wrapped up in the fact that she's a three-month-old yellow lab. Bitsy is a dachshund who wriggles through life with a broken tail. Finally, there's Rex, a cool Australian shepherd mix who is repeating the class. He wears a bandanna around his neck, but if we were all sitting around in some high school study hall, he'd be wearing a leather jacket with a toothpick stored just behind one pointy ear. I instantly have a crush on him on Stella's behalf.

As each person speaks, I'm busy formulating our introduction. The matter of breed is troublesome. All the other dogs have a nice, pat "This is (insert dog's name). He's a (insert dog's breed.) The best I can do for Stella is a laundry list of possible genetic contributors—some kind of cattle dog, maybe a bit of shepherd, a hint of collie, a whisper of beagle. Her docked tail haunts us like a missing clue. The white star on her forehead has long disappeared, overtaken by a brown mask. The majority of her is still a beautiful, glistening black, and the white-spotted breast remains, but as her legs grew long and thin, each developed its own color scheme.

With the exception of Blanca, who is little more than a blond, blurry pompom straining at the end of her leash, all of the other dogs seem remarkably composed. I'm tempted to make rhythmic swishing noises—just to see if I can get Prima and Donna going—but better sense prevails.

In the beginning, Stella had been sitting quietly at my feet, her body one long, quivering shiver against my leg, but as our turn nears, true terror sets in. She rises, plants her front paws on my legs, and looks up into my eyes, pleading with me to take us out of here. Her nails dig into my skin, and I make a mental note not to wear shorts to the next class.

I run through the monologue in my head. *Where to start?*

I'd like her to stop shredding Beanie Babies, to stop eating the cat's food, to stop urinating every time she gets reprimanded, to abandon her excavation project under my youngest son's bed, to allow the occasional new plant to take root in the backyard, to find a source of fiber other than No. 2 pencils, to find some way of showing affection that doesn't include sashaying through the house with a pair of socks or underwear snatched from the hamper.

I just want Stella to be a part of our family. I want a...a...a relationship *with her.*

Instead, when my turn comes, I feel my throat close up as inexplicable tears threaten to spill out of my eyes. "I just want"—I take a deep breath and try again—"I just want Stella to be a part of our family. I want a...a...a *relationship* with her."

There's a moment of silence as everyone wonders when Intermediate Obedience turned into couples' therapy.

"O-kaaaay," Ramon says before deftly spinning my outburst into something upbeat and meaningful. Then it's time for our first lesson: how to settle our dog.

Settling takes time. Quiet time. Ramon suggests about fifteen minutes every day. Shut off the television, ignore the phone, maybe put on some soft music. The idea is to get down on the floor with your dog—let the master go down to where the dog lives—and just be still. Be silent with each other at first, then reach out, pet the dog under its chin, between the shoulder blades, behind the ears in long, soothing strokes until both of you are completely relaxed—synchronized in silent communication. Then, encourage the dog to lie down. Then, to roll over.

That is a settled dog.

Getting a dog to settle in its master's presence is the ultimate demonstration of faith. To settle goes beyond simply sitting or lying down. A settled dog is on its back, belly exposed, mouth slack, ears flopped. A settled dog is not asleep, but fully awake, aware of its vulnerability, completely at ease with its master. A dog that will not settle does not trust. A dog that does not trust will not obey.

"Settled" is not a natural state for Stella.

The first time I try to settle Stella at home, she reacts with all the warmth and affection of an eight-year-old boy forced to endure the annual Christmas kiss from his aunt Edna who always smells of Jergens lotion and tarragon. Stella's brown eyes dart all around the room, looking for an escape, and though she is sitting down, her hind legs are definitely coiled, ready to jump up and take off the minute I move my hand. Her mind seems to be racing with questions: *whatdoesshewant? wherecanigo?whenwillitend?*

Meanwhile, my heart is breaking because all I can see is that she doesn't love me enough—doesn't trust me enough—to simply enjoy a few minutes relaxed in my presence. How can that be? When she was six weeks old, abandoned, alone, didn't I scoop her up, carry her around like a shiny, black bunch of grapes, scared to death to set her down lest some unseen foot accidentally squash her? Don't I provide her with a home, a yard, expensive dog food? Doesn't she have toys—Purple Squeaky Man, Cheeto, and Squirrel—purchased specifically for her entertainment, fetching, and accidental consumption? Have I ever made a sandwich without giving her a slice of cheese? Have I ever denied her the last few drops of my cereal milk?

> *When I see Stella, all I see is Stella, even in those moments when evidence of her sin is everywhere.*

Something happens to me every time I look at this dog. It's the reaction I get when I see those photographs of big-eyed babies curled up in pea pods. It's clichéd and unreasonable, but I melt. Honestly, there's a melting sensation I get—not in my heart, but right at the base of my brain—every time our eyes meet. When I see Stella, *all* I see is

Stella, even in those moments when evidence of her sin is everywhere—a strewn sock, a slightly frayed newspaper, the spot on the carpet that defies all claims of carpet cleaners. All I want in the world is for her to love me enough, trust me enough, to lie down, belly up, and spend a few minutes in mutual adoration.

Why is this so hard?

But I guess it's not that easy for me, either, to spend that quiet time with my Master. Mine is not a naturally settled spirit. Yes, I pray, but I rarely take time to listen past my own voice. I don't take the time simply to be quiet—open and receptive to God's voice. There's something scary in so much stillness.

In Isaiah 30:15, God, a.k.a. the Holy One of Israel, says to His errant people, "In repentance and rest is your salvation, in quietness and trust is your strength, but you would have none of it." Instead, as the chapter goes on to say, the people of Israel listen with their eyes darting around, looking for a means of escape. They want to flee on swift horses, isolating themselves from God's unwarranted protection and love. Their horses will carry them to destruction.

I have swift horses. A stable full of them. I call them appointments and activities—lunch with friends, Bible study, and Tuesday matinées with free popcorn. They are the people I tune in to every afternoon at four o'clock, whose advice fills my ears too full to squeeze in the voice of God. They are self-help books with grinning doctors on the covers, television shows where I vicariously decide who will be top models/singers/designers. They are Internet searches for the perfect summer shoes and endless, yammering conversations where I try to talk myself into finding direction.

I can't imagine there's anything more insulting to God than the fact that I don't spend enough time with Him. I think about the early settling exercises with Stella, where she is so impatiently resistant—like I'm keeping her from some urgent task.

"What else could you possibly have to do?" I ask her, successfully trapping her front paw to prevent her escape. "Is there a squirrel that needs chasing? A sock that needs chewing? A fence board that needs sniffing?" If I have no patience for the activities that tear Stella's attentions away from me, imagine how trivial my daily pursuits must seem to the Creator of the universe.

My Master tells me, "Come to me,…I will give you rest. Take my yoke upon you and learn from me, for I am gentle and humble in heart, and you will find rest for your souls" (Matthew 11:28–29). What could possibly be more wonderful than that? Yet too often my heart is tied up in knots of anxiety and apprehension. Yes, I know the peace of coming alongside Jesus and casting my cares upon Him, but all too often such surrender comes as a final move in some spiritual wrestling match. It's more like giving up or giving in—a surrender that comes to the surface when defeat is imminent. How precious are those times—how much easier is my life—when I settle with Jesus the first time He calls? Jesus is always right there in the middle of my life, waiting for me to come to

> *Jesus is always right there in the middle of my life, waiting for me to come to Him, flop down my heart, and wait, belly up, exposed, ready to roll around in His love for me.*

Him, flop down my heart, and wait, belly up, exposed, ready to roll around in His love for me.

For us, Stella as my delight and I as her master, the only cure for our misunderstanding is time. Every day—several times a day—Stella and I sit together on the floor, just being quiet. Just being still. And settled. At some point, she stops fighting. Stops pulling away.

Now if I sit down on the floor, she actually comes along, flops down without encouragement (or force), and opens herself up to me. If I'm lying on my bed reading or watching TV, she jumps up and lies beside me, stretching companionably.

There was a time when, if I sat next to her as she slept on the couch, my presence would either scare her off to the floor or invite a series of retaliatory snipping. Now, she barely lifts an eyebrow, sighs, and continues her nap—actually scooching a little closer to me. She is the embodiment of the image David creates in Psalm 4:8: "I will lie down and sleep in peace, for you alone, O LORD, make me dwell in safety."

Stella and I are settled.

2

At the Master's Feet

"Sit!"

At your feet they all bow down, and from you
receive instruction.

DEUTERONOMY 33:3

O ur second week at Intermediate Obedience starts off a little better than the first. Stella only tinkles once upon walking into the store and then proceeds of her own free will to our baby-gated classroom. Everybody from the first class has returned, except for Prima and Donna. It's pouring rain outside, and since our last class hadn't specifically targeted their windshield wiper neurosis, I assume their owners opted to spend an afternoon watching home improvement and gardening shows. They seem that type.

I figure we're ahead of the curve when the first lesson that day is teaching our dogs to sit. I mean, come on. Sit? Stella has been sitting forever. Any time I take her out for a walk, I ask her to sit before crossing the street. I insist that she sit before she gets any kind of treat, whether a dog biscuit, a slice of cheese, or the last chicken nugget. Her favorite game is

"Fetch Purple Squeaky Man," and I never throw that toy down the hall until she sits pretty, ready to spring into action and run after it.

So, sit? No problem. Bring it on.

Ramon instructs us to take our dogs to various parts of the store to work on the "Sit!" command. I loop Stella's leash around one of the support columns that run throughout the wide, white aisles so she can't make a straight shot for the door the minute I drop my end. Armed with the desire to prove her well-brought-up nature and a baggie full of treats, I position myself a few feet in front of my darling and face her head-on.

"Sit."

Stella cowers and prances in place—all the while eying the bag of treats.

"C'mon, girl," I say in a higher, sweeter voice. "Sit pretty."

She whines deep within her throat and cranes her head, looking for an escape route behind me.

I can see Ramon making his way from dog to dog—all of which are engaged in one little success story after another. Sit-treat-up-treat. Sit-treat-up-treat. Even Bitsy, the dachshund with the broken tail, is sitting sort of—the best she can given her physical impairment. Ramon is coming closer and closer, and when he's just a few steps away, I give it one last try.

"Sit!"

And the minute Ramon reaches my side, Stella complies, looking nervously from face to face.

"Good girl!" I try not to sound as thrilled and surprised as I feel.

Just as I'm about to give Stella her treat, Ramon stops me.

"Don't reward her until she sits," he says.

Now I'm confused. I look at Stella sitting pretty on the floor in front of me, then at Ramon holding her rapt attention.

"What do you mean? She *is* sitting."

"No," he says. "Look closer."

Following his pointing finger, I examine Stella closely, gazing down her long, lean back to the place where her little tail-nub touches the floor. Then I realize—her little tail-nub *doesn't* touch the floor. It's suspended a good half inch above it, and all four of her legs are quivering as she holds herself in that pose.

It's as if she'd been trained by my grandmother at a road-side rest stop.

"She's just nervous," I explain (as if her shivering self requires explanation). "She sits all the time. When we play fetch, when she gets snacks…"

And that's the problem. Every time Stella sits, she's anticipating the next "big thing." She needs to learn to sit for sitting's sake.

Jesus knew the importance of sitting. Consider the time He faced the crowd of hungry people, having nothing more than a few loaves of bread and two fish to feed them. No doubt He knew the miracle that was about to occur, but the crowd didn't. Nothing can rouse a group of people to a collective panic state like five thousand grumbling stomachs. So, what did He do? He told the people to sit down, then He took just five little loaves of bread and two fish, said a blessing, and fed the entire crowd with that meal (see Matthew 14:18–19).

This story is often used as an illustration of Jesus' divine ability to perform a miracle, but there are really two miracles here. Of course, the supernatural multiplication of a boy's sack lunch is one, but let's not overlook the fact that, through a simple request, Jesus was able to get five thousand people to sit. What better picture could we have of His authority? The crowd could not have anticipated that lunch was coming; after all, they only saw five little loaves and two fish. Had they the idea that this meager amount of food was destined to feed them all, human nature dictates that those little loaves and fish would have been snatched out of the Savior's hands in a matter of seconds. No, they sat simply because He told them to.

I have a feeling that He had no intention of feeding anybody until all five thousand people were sitting quietly. They obeyed, and they were rewarded—not just with food (though for some that would be enough), but with the privilege of being witness to one of the greatest miracles ever performed. Additionally, their obedience set them up to hear more of the Master's teaching. The crowd was sitting and sated. They were ready to learn.

According to Ramon, if I never get Stella to sit, we'll never progress to more complex behaviors. In fact, as far as Intermediate Obedience is concerned, failure to master sitting basically means kissing good-bye the next five weeks' instruction. A dog that will not sit will not walk. A dog that will not sit will not stay. Where settling your dog puts her in the position of trust, getting her to sit puts her in the position of obedience.

We had some work to do, and it would start with Stella and I both correcting some bad habits.

In the past, when I had wanted Stella to sit, I would say something like, "Come on, pretty girl! Sit pretty! Come on, sweetie. Sit down! Sit pretty!" Ramon pointed out that in doing so I was giving her three separate commands: come; sit; down. And of course Stella, my Mensa-candidate canine, was confused. That would explain her agitated state whenever I told her to sit.

Sit? Okay. What? No? Come? Okay. What? No? Sit? Okay. What? No? Down? Okay...

As her master, I need to keep my commands simple.

When Jesus wanted the crowd to sit before He fed them, He didn't wander among them saying, "Hey, we're going to have lunch in a few minutes, so could you go ahead and have a seat? Guys? Could you come over here and sit down? We're just... Excuse me, people? Do you mind? If I could get everybody to find a rock..."

> We had some work to do, and it would start with Stella and I both correcting some bad habits.

No. He stood on the hillside—somewhere above them where everybody could see Him—and merely said, "Sit." In fact, I imagine Him doing a sweeping hand motion along with it. "Sit."

Once we're home from class, Stella and I start our new sitting regime. First, we spend a little time settling together, then I take my place on our living room sofa and break out the treats—a handful of dog biscuits broken into countless little pieces.

That gets her attention.

"Stella?" I use the voice that hostage negotiators always use in the movies. "Sit."

She looks at me, then at the treat, and sits. But it's her old sit, with her tail-nub hovering. I know this because I've leaned over to check. Ever watchful, Stella follows my movement, craning her own neck down and around to check her own tail-nub. She sees nothing wrong with it, as evidenced by its nervous little wiggle at the end of her spine, so she looks up at me again, expecting a treat.

I ignore her, and after a few seconds she gets up and saunters over to sniff my hand.

"Uh, uh," I say. "Sit." The "uh, uh" sound isn't your average negative noise. To reproduce it accurately, you'd need to get a four-year-old to ride a Big Wheel through moist gravel. Quite unpleasant indeed.

Once again she complies; once again our heads move in perfect synchronicity, turning and craning to see if she's given me a true sit, or a Stella sit. Once again the nub hovers, and I ignore her until she stands up and takes a step toward the hand with the treat.

"Uh, uh. Sit."

This time my command is different. I reach out with my free hand and point—over her body—to her nub and down. As if I'm willing it to the ground through the sheer force of my suspended finger. If my hand were a bony claw, you'd think I was playing the part of the Ghost of Christmas Future in some living room production of *A Christmas Carol*.

And Stella sits.

We both check her nub, and it's solidly on the ground. She's sitting—truly sitting—and I give her a treat.

"Good girl!" I say. Then I pat my leg to release her from sitting, and we start all over again. Two or three more tries, and she no longer gets a treat. Her only reward for sitting is my praise. After a while the verbal command is superfluous; Stella's nub hits the floor the moment I point to it.

When Jesus asks us to sit, He wants our nubs on the floor. The gospel of Luke records a visit He made to the home of two sisters, Mary and Martha. While Martha is fluttering around, "distracted by all the preparations that had to be made," Mary sits at the Lord's feet, hanging on to His every word. When Martha complains, urging Jesus to tell Mary to get up and help out a little, Jesus says, "Martha, Martha,…you are worried and upset about many things, but only one thing is needed. Mary has chosen what is better, and it will not be taken away from her" (Luke 10:38–42).

> *When Jesus asks us to sit, He wants our nubs on the floor.*

Suppose Jesus had asked Martha to come in and sit. No doubt she would have complied, but would she truly sit? I picture Mary, fully on the floor at the feet of Jesus, her robe puddled around her on the ground. But Martha? She'd probably bring in some little chore—some fruit to peel or dice. She'd be more likely to perch than to sit, balancing her busy little nub on the edge of a stool so she could hop right up the minute something needed to be pulled out of the oven or spooned into a bowl.

I don't think Mary sat in obedience to any command. Jesus didn't have a bag of treats to reward her, and He didn't praise her directly. He was simply present. He had something to say, and Mary knew the only way to hear it was to sit at His feet.

Jesus doesn't have to come and sit on my couch to let me know He has something to say. Psalm 119:89 says, "Your word, O LORD, is eternal; it stands firm in the heavens." Jesus has had a word for me every minute of every day throughout my life, but I haven't always been willing to sit—really sit—and listen. I spent many years in church with my nub on the pew and my mind just about anywhere else. I could flip through my Bible, my eyes zipping from one underlined passage to another, never bothering to think there might be much worth reading in between. I stayed away from any opportunity for deep instruction, figuring it would be wasted time on a hill when I had so many other things I could be doing in my kitchen. I spent twenty years fluttering in and out of His presence because I simply wasn't willing to stop, sit, and study everything He wanted to teach me.

I could take a lesson from Stella's cousin, Elle.

My sister, Barbara, has a beautiful shepherd mix named Elle who had been shuffled from home to home, often neglected and abused. When Barbara first took Elle in, the dog alternated between cowering at a distance and bursting with hyperenthusiastic attack. I'd heard stories about Elle—the black and tan whirlwind that would take off across the vast Wyoming plains at the first whiff of a rabbit—but it would be a couple of years before I had the chance to visit and meet her for myself.

And what a surprise awaits me once I get there.

After the initial jump-and-sniff greeting, Elle displays a most pleasant canine presence. I notice she never lets my sister get more than a few steps away from her, but when Barbara and I settle down for a long, summer afternoon chat, I see the extent of Elle's devotion. The moment Barbara takes a seat, Elle reclines on her feet. Not *at* her feet, but directly *on* them. My sister is buried up to her ankles in dark black fur.

"How did you get her to do that?" I ask.

"She just does it," Barbara says. "It's fine as long as you don't want to move."

Sometimes that's the point. Not moving.

3

The Best-Laid Plans

"Down!"

Many are the plans in a man's heart, but it is the
LORD's purpose that prevails.

PROVERBS 19:21

*N*o sooner has Stella proven her ability to "Sit!" when Ramon says it's time to move on to "Down!" And this is a whole new beast. I can instruct Stella to sit from three feet away. From across the room, eventually. But "Down!" calls for a different level of closeness.

We stay in our quiet corner at the back of the store, right by the expensive self-cleaning litter boxes. Then she sits. What a pretty girl. Here's a treat. But there's a twist. I approach Stella with another treat, fully displayed in my open hand, and— *boom*! I close my fist and hold it just an inch away from her nose. She knows it's there. In fact, she stretches her long neck out until her nose bumps up against my balled fingers.

"Down!" I tell her, lowering my hand toward the floor. Stella continues to bump her nose against my hand—the impatient little nudge an attempt to pry my fingers open. To release the treat before its time. But my fingers don't budge. Instead, I continue down, down, down until my fist is on the tile. Soon Stella's head is on the floor too. Unfortunately, her legs aren't. Neither is her chest. Or her belly. She's basically sitting, head stretched to the floor, licking my hand and becoming more frustrated with each attempt. In fact, she gets so irritated, she forgets my earlier command.

She stands.

"Uh, uh," I say in the ugly voice, and we have to start all over. In less than a minute we're right back where we were. She's craning and straining, and there's nothing I can do to make her understand what I want, short of yanking her legs out from underneath her. After all, Ramon has said that sometimes we have to use hands-on obedience, but it's a last resort. If I do that, it won't be Stella learning on her own. So she fusses. And nudges. And stands…again.

"Uh, uh." The ugly sound returns.

I've kept the same treat in my hand since our first attempt. Now my palm is sweaty. I can feel the grainy crumbs of the biscuit between my fingers, and thanks to Stella's persistence, the rest of my hand is just as soggy. But I offer my best smile-at-Stella voice and tell her one more time, "Sit!"

She sits.

Again the fist. Again the sniffs. I look over my shoulder to see if the watchful eyes of Ramon are anywhere near. Nope—I can hear him lavishing praise on that dull-witted Bitsy, the broken-tailed dachshund. Of course *she* will lie down on command. After all, standing can be so exhausting. Meanwhile, Stella's beginning to nudge in earnest, but before she can stand up again, I grab her front paws with my free hand and give a swift little yank.

And "Down!" she goes.

Because sometimes a master just has to get a girl's attention.

Once when I was at a summer youth church camp, God yanked my paws out from under me. My friend Stacey had broken her foot playing tennis and wasn't due to have the cast removed until a week after camp was over. As much as she tried to convince her doctor to take it off early, he'd refused. It was the summer before our senior year—our last chance to be at camp together. After one disastrous attempt to wrap the cast in trash bags so Stacey could take a shower, we decided to take it off ourselves.

Yes, we. As in Stacey, my friends Nan and Elaine, and me. Not a medical degree among us, and truth be told, probably a collective seventy-eight average in science. But we wanted to go on prayer walks. We wanted to hike down to the creek. We wanted to sneak out in the dewy nights to meet the cute boys from the other churches. We wanted to nudge the camp rules aside with our wet little noses.

So one night, armed with nothing more than adolescent shortsightedness and a pair of nail scissors, we went to work.

Little by little, we moistened the cast and snipped away the soggy plaster. One of us stood as lookout while the other two toiled away. It was nearly two o'clock in the morning when Stacey's shriveled, rather stinky foot finally broke free, and we snuck back to our bunks, full of self-congratulatory praise.

> *Sometimes a master just has to get a girl's attention.*

Now we'll be able to take the shortcut to the dining hall. Nudge.

Now we'll be able to partner up for the obstacle course. Nudge.

Then, after a moment of silence, we have one more revelation. A voice coming from the bunk above me. Stacey only brought one shoe.

All eight legs in one fell swoop.

Of course, we weren't the first fools to rest our heads, stare into the dark, and charge forth in planning a future. Jesus tells the story of the rich fool (see Luke 12:16–21). Here was a man blessed with a big harvest and an even bigger problem—where to put it all. But every problem has a solution, so he snuggled down into his pillow and came up with a plan to build bigger barns to hold it all. Granted, his idea seems like a logical step, but there's one problem. It's *his* idea. He's looking at the possibilities—the days ahead and the rewards within the closed fist of the future. The rich fool's plans for the bigger barns? That's his first nudge. But, like Stella, he's not content to stop there.

He says to himself, "You have plenty of good things laid up for many years." Nudge. "Take life easy." Nudge. "Eat, drink, and be merry."

Nudge. Nudge. Nudge.

All in a night's conversation, and a one-way conversation at that. But then things take a very different turn when the voice of God comes down from the ultimate top bunk.

"You fool!" God says to him in the darkness. "This very night your life will be demanded from you. Then who will get what you have prepared for yourself?"

Even flat in bed, his legs were knocked out from underneath him.

Whether one rich fool or four young ones, I don't think it's a coincidence that the moment of knee-jerk reality comes late in the still, dark night. I'm teaching Stella to get "Down!" in preparation for a time when I'm going to need to get a handle on her behavior in some canine crisis. Like a stranger at the door. Or a new dog passing on the block. Basically a situation when I need to save her from herself.

Just like Stella's not really sitting until she's nub-down on the floor, she's not lying down until she's completely off her feet. That means front legs stretched out straight in front, and back legs shifted off to the side. Otherwise, she's just one spring away from being "Up!" "Down!" is a pose that intends to keep her in her place for a while—still and ready for the next meaningful instruction.

Once I finally yank Stella's legs and get her in the right pose, I open my hand and let her lick the soggy remains of the crumbled biscuit—nothing like the fresh and crispy reward I wanted to give her. I'm offering it to her out of a grudging sense of obligation (to have it licked from between my fingers, mostly), so there's none of the joy that usually comes when I toss her a treat.

Now, it's hard to look at the Parable of the Rich Fool and see the announcement of one's impending death as any kind of a treat. But it's not the news itself that makes it unpalatable; it's the nudging buildup of nonsense that precedes it. Imagine if he'd gone to bed, exhausted from a long day's work bringing his abundant harvest to his waiting barns. If he'd simply responded to the Master's command, instilled in the natural rhythm of his body. If he'd looked into the darkness, motionless and quiet.

God still might have opened His hand, but imagine how different the revelation would be. It wouldn't change the man's fate. His life would still end that night. But how much sweeter would it be to go out with a spirit of satisfaction. With an affectionate scratch behind the ears and praise for a job well done—a life well lived.

Lying down means surrendering. Giving up control. Handing everything over including when—or if—or how—to get up again. And why not hand it over to the One who holds everything in His hand?

To date, this is the most difficult behavior for Stella to master, and she's not the only one. Bitsy, the broken-tailed dachshund, takes right to it, but I don't admire her motivation. She has an overwhelming passivity—a dullness that seems to translate to, "Sure. Down? Why not?" Rex also has no problem, but he's not passive. He's just cool. Blanca has everybody fooled because, frankly, she's cheating. She hasn't shifted her legs, and she's ready to pounce, but I can't bring myself to rat out a puppy. Prima and Donna aren't here for this lesson, but I can't imagine it would go well.

At first I attribute Stella's trouble to her fearful nature. She is always wary, always shirking and slinking and shaking. Always worrying. But now I can see the darker side to this weakness—a certain nefarious spin to what once gave me a fierce desire to protect her. She doesn't want to lie down because she doesn't want to give in. The longer she's head up, nub on the floor, paws on the ground, she's in charge. She has power. She's her own master.

Lying down means surrendering. Giving up control. Handing everything over including when—or if—or how—to get up again. And why not hand it over to the One who holds everything in His hand?

James says it straight out. "Now listen, you who say, 'Today or tomorrow we will go to this or that city, spend a year there, carry on business and make money.' Why, you do not even know what will happen tomorrow. What is your life? You are a mist that appears for a little while and then vanishes" (4:13–14).

I know Stella isn't sneaking around planning some sort of future outside my realm of influence. Dogs have no concept of the future. Not tomorrow, not later this afternoon, not even the next five minutes. She only knows *now*. This minute.

She is a constant mental mist; her thoughts form and dissipate almost simultaneously.

As limited as I am in my humanity, my perception is infinite compared to hers. She doesn't know her future. I do, at least as far as God allows me to. I know all kinds of things she doesn't—beginning with what's in my hand. She's just as likely to nudge at an empty fist as one holding a moist, crumbling treat. She can't understand that "Down!" for now doesn't mean "Down!" forever.

In the meantime, when I'm "Down!"—face, feet, and belly on the floor—I need to remember that God will lift me up *in due time* (see 1 Peter 5:6).

In other words, I should stop nudging.

4

A Bird in the Mouth

"Drop It!"

Your eyes are too pure to look on evil;
you cannot tolerate wrong.

HABAKKUK 1:13

At any given time, Stella has something in her mouth. Sometimes it's one of her legitimate toys—Purple Squeaky Man, Cheeto, or Squirrel—but nothing is off limits. I've seen her trotting through the house carrying everything from history homework to Q-tips. Most often, her cargo is innocuous—a stray sock or a tattered tennis ball. But sometimes she clamps her jaws around something valuable, like a jump drive that contains the entire manuscript of my second novel.

Before going to Intermediate Obedience, getting Stella to let go of anything clenched in her mouth followed a predictable pattern.

Step One: Realize that Stella has closed her teeth around contraband—let's say a stray sock.

Step Two: Scream, "Stella! Give that to me!"

Step Three: Give chase.

Step Four: Confront.

Step Five: Take sock away.

Step Six: Clean carpet.

At some point, I find myself looking down at Stella who is, in turn, looking up at me, eyes locked with mine in a terror-filled gaze.

I want to keep this. I found it. It's mine.

Unwilling to relinquish her prize, her lip curls over the mouthful of white cotton and she breathes through her nose, making a whistling sound of sorts. The moment of truth comes as soon as I bend down to take said foreign object away, because that's when I realize that Stella is about to submit. Not surrender, submit. Oh, she recognizes my authority, and she knows exactly what I want her to do. Rather than dropping whatever treasure she found, however, she assumes that dreaded, familiar squatting pose.

"No, Stella! Don't—" But it's too late. Like a scene from some twisted cartoon, she's gone, still clutching the contraband, and I'm left with a tiny piddle right at, or on, my feet.

She doesn't understand why I care. I have no better use for an empty granola bar wrapper, so why should I care that she fished it out of the trash? If my sons leave the crayons on the floor, why should she be the one to get in trouble when the cerulean blue finds its way into her mouth? With the exception of one incident involving a razor plucked from the edge of the bathtub, the tidbits she ferries from place to place pose no threat to herself or to others. So why should she drop it?

Because, be it trash or treasure, it's mine—and I want her to drop it.

On the third Saturday of Intermediate Obedience, I bring Stella's Cheeto to class and let her hold it in her mouth, play with it, carry it all over the store—anything she fancies. While much of her nervousness has worn down, she is still seized with a perpetual underlying spirit of fear. Having her Cheeto is supposed to bring comfort. A bit of home.

And then I take it away.

Persuading a dog to "Drop It!" is essentially a trade. After allowing Stella to bound happily through the store with Cheeto clasped in her jaws, I call her to me and command her to sit. Then comes a Hollywood moment: Stella's choice.

For today's class, we've been told not only to bring one of our dog's beloved treasures, but also an extra-special treat. Normally I bring a baggie full of broken biscuits, which our family with its macabre sense of humor has dubbed "bone chips." But today I've gone all-out. I have a bag of "fakon"— imitation, bacon-flavored-looks-like-real-bacon snack strips.

Stella is absolutely crazy about this treat. At home, we

have to keep them in triple-sealed plastic bags. She knows they're in my backpack; she's been sniffing at it and eying me suspiciously since we got in the car. Maybe that's why she was so good about actually getting into class today—walking straight into the store, no dragging, no piddling. She must have been thinking, *Woo-hoo! Today we bring out the big treats!*

And, really, I'd love to give her one right now, but it seems her mouth is full. I pull one little strip out of the bag, hold it out, and say, "Drop it!"

There's no way she can keep Cheeto *and* get the fakon; for Stella, there's not even a moment's hesitation. I could have sworn I heard a *ptooey* sound as Cheeto, the beloved orange fuzzy bone, hit the ground like a watermelon seed at a church picnic.

Before Stella knew to anticipate the reward that comes with obedience, we had a few wrestling matches where I chased her, pinned her down, pried her jaws apart, and yanked away whatever offending object I'd deemed too dangerous or too valuable for her consumption. We'd both leave those encounters exhausted and more than a little unhappy with each other. I'd be covered in dog hair and spittle; she'd feel frightened and confused. After all, compared to her, I'm a giant with power and resources that she can't fathom. I have a keener sense of cause and effect, but when we're locked in that kind of struggle, she has no idea how much I have her best interest at heart.

Some things just aren't worth holding on to.

I've noticed that, as I'm trying to carry everything this life has given me, my Master has asked me to drop a lot of things. Anybody who drops by my house unexpectedly might think I received a divine command to drop housework and laundry, but my weaknesses there have no heavenly directive. But dropping my job? That's a different story.

> *I could have sworn I heard a* ptooey *sound as Cheeto, the beloved orange fuzzy bone, hit the ground like a watermelon seed at a church picnic.*

I graduated from high school, went to college, and went straight back to high school, following a lifelong dream to become a high school English teacher. Other little girls want to be princesses and ballerinas, but I wanted to be Karen Valentine from the television show *Room 222*. (Technically, she wasn't an English teacher, but I was more interested in having the miniskirt and yellow Volkswagen Bug anyway.) As it turned out, I loved teaching every bit as much as I thought I would. I felt fulfilled and happy for seventeen years. I knew I was pursuing the career the Lord intended for me, and I left campus most days with the perfect blend of satisfaction and exhaustion. My colleagues were my friends; my students were my kids. I was respected and revered in the only profession I had ever wanted.

Then I wrote my first book.

In some ways, embarking on a writing career was like meeting Jesus for the first time all over again. Like Simon and Andrew, James and John—four happy fishermen called from their boats to become disciples of Jesus Christ (see Matthew 4:18–22). Doubtless they knew who Jesus was, had listened to His message, maybe kept His truths tucked away in the back of their minds every day when they set out to sea. Who knows how many mornings He may have strolled along the shore, wishing them a good day in the morning or inquiring about the day's haul in the evening. Jesus was a part of their lives in a very real way before they ever dropped their nets to heed His command, "Follow Me." When they did, everything about their relationships changed.

They never looked back, and neither did I.

Make no mistake, I loved teaching and identifying myself as a teacher. I measured my years from August to August. But midway into the first semester one year, Jesus said, "Drop it." He allowed me to hold on to the joy as I fulfilled my final contract, but I lived each day with a gentle, authoritative command.

"Drop it."

I had to relinquish my Cheeto, step out of my boat, and obey.

It's a sopping, soggy Saturday in San Antonio—one of those days when it seems like God is dropping buckets of water from the sky. It's not really a storm; there's no dramatic display of thunder or lightning. It's just a constant, solid downpour.

And it's been going on for days.

The entire backyard is nothing but a series of muddy puddles. We've given up trying to wipe Stella's paws off each time she comes inside. It'll be easier to let it all dry up and vacuum it later. Looking at the accumulation of paw prints by the door, we seem to be only a few steps shy of a Seurat-like masterpiece.

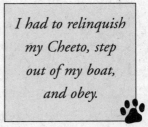

I had to relinquish my Cheeto, step out of my boat, and obey.

We are all gathered in the living room watching a family-friendly movie when Stella makes it known that she needs to go outside. She doesn't run to the door and scratch; she doesn't stroll to the door and sit. She doesn't go to the door at all. Instead, she plants her front paws on the arm of the couch and stands, stretching to her fullest height, then draws her face close, close, close to mine.

Hey, buddy. Outside.

If I try to ignore her, she'll lean closer, plunk her paws onto my legs, and walk them up my chest until they rest on my shoulders—and her wet, cold nose brushes my cheek.

It's my turn to let her out, and the second I open the french door, she's gone like a shot, tearing down the little path she's worn between the porch and the back fence. She makes tiny mud splashes as she runs, and I cringe just thinking about the mess she's going to track back inside.

I know better than to sit back down while she's outside. Her attention span is miniscule even in fair weather, and I know she'll want to come back in before I hit the couch. So I stand at the door and watch her run along the length of the back fence before slowly making her way back to the porch. But something catches her attention, and soon she's nuzzling around in the wet grass. She lifts her head, takes a step back, then lowers her nose to the ground again. I can't tell what she has discovered. It's getting dark outside, and the rain obscures practically everything, but as she makes her happy, trotting way back to the house, her new treasure takes shape.

It's a bird. And it's dead.

All my training on how to be a good master flies out the window as I scream, "Stella's got a bird!" (Well, in my mind that's what I screamed, but my husband assures me I was spouting barely intelligible, hysterical vowel sounds.) At any rate, my voice must have been loud enough to carry through the door, because Stella looks absolutely terrified once she steps onto the porch. She clamps her mouth around that sodden, lifeless body and paces in nervous circles on the other side of the door.

Then my husband does the unthinkable. He strides to the door and opens it wide. There, on the other side of the threshold, is Stella, holding tight to a mass of soggy mud and feathers. Mikey, however, holds an entire bacon treat—the expensive kind we only dole out in ripped-up bits.

Even from my vantage point as I cower behind the couch, I can see Stella assessing the situation. I can't imagine that the bird in her mouth gives her any satisfaction; it's just something new and different. Something she stumbled upon. Something that captured her curiosity. But she can't bring it inside, because Mike stands in the doorway. What she holds is awful; what Mike holds is delicious. She can't have both.

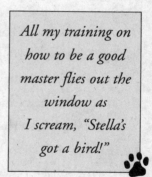

All my training on how to be a good master flies out the window as I scream, "Stella's got a bird!"

"Drop it." My husband delivers an utterly calm command.

Ptooey.

Stella pads inside, accepts the fakon trade, and one of my

boys wraps her in the large, soft beach towel we keep near the door before he whisks her away to the bathroom where another boy is charged with brushing her teeth.

But the story's not quite over. There's still the matter of the bird.

This is where Mike, the master of the house, shows himself to be a true, loving master to Stella, like the one described in Psalm 103:9–12:

He will not always accuse,
　　nor will he harbor his anger forever;
he does not treat us as our sins deserve
　　or repay us according to our iniquities.
For as high as the heavens are above the earth,
　　so great is his love for those who fear him;
as far as the east is from the west,
　　so far has he removed our transgressions from us.

Earthly physics prevent us from removing the bird as far as the east is from the west, but it is bundled into three layers of grocery bags, tied tight, dropped into a larger trash bag, tied tighter, and tossed over the fence into the alley. As far as Stella is concerned, that's where the world stops.

What she's dropped has been forgotten.

5

Yours, Mine, and...Well, Mine

"Leave It!"

The LORD gave and the LORD has taken away;
may the name of the LORD be praised.

JOB 1:21

*R*amon may be the instructor for the Saturday afternoon Intermediate Obedience class, but his dog, Reese, is the star. Reese is a ninety-five-pound golden labrador retriever who often makes an appearance during class. He comes out to serve as a model and inspiration to the rest of us, who could only hope to have a dog as responsive and compliant as he is. If we were holding class in a lecture hall rather than in a circle of baby gates in a pet store, Ramon would be the professor commanding our attention at center stage, and Reese would be the thirty-four-year-old grad student in an ill-fitting sweater, meandering up and down the rows handing back blue books. Of course, this would only happen if Ramon gave the command, "Meander!"

But right now, Reese sits perfectly still at his master's feet while our dogs respond in their individual, psychosis-fed ways. Prima and Donna, the hyper Yorkshire terriers, spin in little circles in their owners' laps. Three-month-old Blanca is held at bay as her puppy paws tread the tiles in a frantic Scooby-like run. Bitsy's little broken tail is whipping away, but that's the dachshund's only acknowledgment of Reese's presence. Rex, the Australian shepherd mix, is equally cool, giving Reese a little doggy nod and a veiled challenge to race him in the abandoned quarry at midnight, man.

Stella trembles. I wouldn't classify her reaction as outright fear—Reese is about as threatening as Peter O'Toole. Rather, it's a trembling that comes over her as a result of being in Reese's very presence, like Stella's his biggest fan and can't believe he's right here. So close. She alternates between straining at her leash and clinging to my leg. I whisper in her ear, reassuring her that she's just as wonderful as Reese is, but she won't look me in the eye.

She doesn't believe me.

Reese, meanwhile, barely acknowledges our presence. He doesn't so much as raise an eyebrow, even as Blanca—the younger, female version of himself—is engaged in a frantic display of "Look at Me!" I get the distinct impression that we all could be covered in barbeque sauce and set on fire, and Reese would do little more than yawn and scoot an inch away from the flames to keep his tail from getting singed.

Then, that very tail makes a barely perceptible thump on the floor. Something has captured his attention.

Ramon has reached inside Reese's open kennel and taken out an object familiar to almost any dog owner. The foot-long hunk of thick rope in Ramon's hand is knotted at each end, frayed, and discolored—obviously the result of countless hours of playing tug and chew and fetch. Every dog in class perks up at its appearance; even Reese's eyes flash a bit of a light as our instructor walks the perimeter of our little circle, waving the tug-toy in the air.

"Who do you think this belongs to?" he asks.

Ever the teacher's pet, I throw my hand in the air and call out the answer. "Reese!"

"Wrong!" says Ramon, with an irritating hint of triumph. He adds insult by gesturing with the toy itself, so all eyes— canine and human—shift toward me. I'm ready to crawl inside Stella's skin and sulk out of here. "This," he continues, "belongs to me. I allow Reese to play with it, but it belongs to me. Reese lives in my house. I'm the master. Everything belongs to me."

He brings the ratty, saliva-soaked end of the rope right up to the tip of Reese's nose, and the dog gazes at it with a subtle longing. Ramon actually taps the tip of the nose and still no response. Then, he tosses the toy down. The minute it hits the floor, Ramon makes a sweeping motion with his hand and says, "Leave it!"

A treasure is mere inches away, yet Reese doesn't move.

For this particular lesson, we have brought Cheeto—a small, bone-shaped, stuffed toy covered in soft, orange fur. It squeaks when you squeeze it, and that squeaking sound will bring Stella running from the farthest corners of the house or yard. At Ramon's command, I hold it in my hand and tell myself over and over, "This is mine." It's matted, it smells weird, and it's mine. I have absolutely no need for it. My life would not change one iota if it were to disappear from the face of the earth.

Still, it's mine.

I remember the day it came into existence. Not when it was manufactured, but when its presence became meaningful. It was the day Stella and I came into each other's lives. I remember driving to Wal-Mart in the car God allows me to use, buying it with the money He allows me to earn. Cheeto was twice the size of Stella's head back then, and nothing could have been more fun than seeing what pleasure she took from that toy. She loved it at first squeak, and I took great delight in watching that love.

I gave this prized possession to Stella the day she became

my dog, but I didn't fully become her master until the day we both learned that I could take it away.

I live a life surrounded by treasures, and they all have my mark on them. My house is a messy conglomeration of books and shoes and little bouquets. My car? Swap shoes for sweaters, and it's the same. Every tangible thing I need and love in life is within my reach. Always. I like to think that I've worked hard for it all. That I deserve it. It's easy to acknowledge God's sovereign ownership of the roof over my head but more difficult to extend that concept to everything underneath it. God, however, has no problem claiming it at all.

> I have no need of a bull from your stall
>> or of goats from your pens,
> for every animal of the forest is mine,
>> and the cattle on a thousand hills.
> I know every bird in the mountains,
>> and the creatures of the field are mine.
>> (Psalm 50:9–11)

The earth is one big home, with God keenly aware of every bit of it. There's nothing, not the tiniest mustard seed–sized object that escapes His cognizance. Everything I have is a direct result of the life He allows me to live. I'm simply playing with the toys He left out for me. So why do I still classify things as *mine*?

Meanwhile, Stella takes my sovereignty for granted. She plays tug with Cheeto; she fetches Cheeto. She carries it around all day long and curls up with it when she naps. But sometimes Cheeto disappears. It might get nudged under a couch, tossed behind a bookcase, lost within a basket of laundry. Oddly enough, when this happens, Stella doesn't spend days—or hours—moping around, looking for her lost treasure, even as much as she loves it. She simply turns her attention to one of the other toys I've provided—Purple Squeaky Man or Squirrel. She plays with and fetches those with the same spirit of contentment as she would with Cheeto. Then, when I move the couch to vacuum, or when I put away the laundry, or peer behind the bookcase and reunite her with her treasure, I'm as delighted to see her joy as I was the first time I gave it to her.

God reminds me of His sovereignty in this area every day, often through tragedy. I've seen them on the news—families who have lost everything. Homes washed away by flood, swept away by tornado, or burned to the ground by fire. People lose sons and daughters in war and their parents to disease. Companies go bankrupt, and men and women can't feed their families. Predators invade and children disappear. It's hard to look at such tragedies and believe that God is in control, but He is.

One late afternoon in August 2005, my older brother, Chris, died. Or, as we like to say, God took him home. That's the beautiful picture—the one of our heavenly Father bringing one of His children home to Himself, but there's the undeniable other side to it. My brother is gone. Our parents lost a son, his wife lost her husband, and two children lost their father. One would think that our lives would fall apart at his passing. But they didn't. We didn't. We took comfort in the other bits of our world that God allows us to have. The truth of His promises. The love we share with one another. *One another.*

> *There's nothing equal about a human life and a home, or a home and a job, or a job and a child— except in this: all are gifts from God.*

There's nothing equal about a human life and a home, or a home and a job, or a job and a child—except in this: all are gifts from God. He allows people to come in and out of our lives, and all who recognize Him as Savior get to claim an eternal connection that reaches far beyond these fleeting, earthbound years.

As for our possessions—nothing gets a classification higher than "trinket" in God's eyes. All those things we work so hard for, pay so much money for, and use to measure our power and success? None of them are of any more value to God than Stella's Cheeto is to me.

And yet He holds them all, just as I hold this orange fuzzy thing, sitting in class, coming to grips for the first time with a master's true authority.

Initially, teaching a dog to "Leave It!" seems cruel. Like teasing. I begin by holding a treat in my hand—right under Stella's nose. The minute she tries to take the treat, I close my hand and say, "Leave it!" I keep my fingers wrapped as Stella nudges and paws at my fist. Only when she loses interest and gives up do I open my hand, offer the treat and say, "Take it!" To my surprise, by the third repetition Stella has learned not to nudge, and the next time I don't have to close my hand at all. The treat simply rests in my palm, undisturbed, until I give her permission to "Take It!"

Then we ramp it up. I put the treat on the floor in front of her. Deep down inside, I want her to obey with the placid dignity of Reese. Instead, she snags it off the floor before I can even finish telling her to leave it there. I give her the ugly, "Uh, uh," but she's already chomped it down.

So, we start again. This time she ignores my closed hand on the first try, and maybe it's my imagination, but I sense a touch of humility when I allow her to take the treat. Two or three more successes and I ramp it up again, telling her to "Leave It!" as I drop the treat on the floor. As an added measure, I imitate Ramon's Jedi-like gesture by waving my hand over it as I repeat the command. Now, it's not that I don't want Stella to have the treat, I just want her to learn that she doesn't get to have it just because it's there. She gets to have it because—and when—I say so. The objective isn't to give her the treat, it's to get her to give up the desire. To be willing to go on without it.

Every Saturday on our way to Intermediate Obedience, Stella and I drive through a neighborhood full of beautiful, sprawling homes. I don't have to take this route. I could stay on the highway and take the access road exit. But I like to drive this way. Some of these are stately, three-story, red-brick minimansions. Others have a rough-hewn stone facade. Circular driveways host multiple shiny, new cars; the lawns are manicured and landscaped to perfection. I imagine the rooms inside.

Shining hardwood floors, marble countertops, stainless-steel appliances, the perfect balance of antiques and contemporary styles. These are homes where voices echo, where people bathe in Jacuzzi tubs.

Block after block I hear my Master saying, "Leave it. Leave it. Leave it." These are treasures He holds in His hand, and there had been a time I persistently nudged around, trying to get at them. Not seriously—I wasn't consulting Realtors or anything—but my mind and heart were in a constant state of dissatisfaction. My fixation on owning a home in this neighborhood blinded me to the blessings of that very moment: driving in an almost-paid-for mini-van, listening to a CD of disco tunes downloaded and burned by a husband who loves me and knows how to do such things.

> *As for our possessions— nothing gets a classification higher than "trinket" in God's eyes.*

I'm not teaching Stella to "Leave It!" simply to delay inevitable gratification. The key to the behavior is to break the fixation. No dog ever truly obeys this command until she completely walks away from whatever was being denied. You want your dog to know this command for those times when she's sniffing at the poisonous plant in your home or the undesirable *blech* you pass on your daily walk. This is what you call out just before the dog picks up the fallen baby toy or snatches the leftover ham from the kitchen counter—even if you fully intend to make part of that ham a snack later on.

I want Stella to know that no distraction is worth disobedience. If she walks away from temptation, she enters a world full of wonderful things at her disposal. These days I can put a cheeseburger on the floor in front of Stella, wave my hand, say "Leave it!" and as long as I remain next to her, she'll leave it

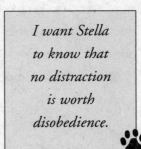

I want Stella to know that no distraction is worth disobedience.

alone. She doesn't ignore it completely. At first she'll fidget and whine; she might even make a move toward it and make me repeat the command. But eventually her wonderfully short attention span kicks in, and she wanders off. She'll take a bite out of her food dish or pick up a toy. She might saunter to the door and request a romp outside. And who knows? I might call her back immediately and give her the burger. Or I might put it away for another time. I might even seal it in a plastic bag, put it in the trash, and toss the trash over the fence into the alley, getting rid of it forever.

It's my choice. My decision.

My love for her isn't wrapped up in that cheeseburger. My

love is in the home I provide, in all the things she can take for granted. It's in the toys she can pick up and play with at will, the food that magically appears in her dish every day, the heartworm pill she takes every month. It's in the open end of the couch when she wants to take a nap, the yard with the sturdy fence to keep other big, mean dogs away, and the leash that holds us together when we venture out into the neighborhood.

Psalm 16:5–6 says:

> LORD, you have assigned me my portion and my cup;
> you have made my lot secure.
> The boundary lines have fallen for me in pleasant places;
> surely I have a delightful inheritance.

I can provide all of these things for Stella, my beloved, because God has provided all of them for me. I live within boundaries forged by budget and economy and choice and time. But my boundaries are infinitely pleasant ones. There are wonderful, arbitrary distractions out there, but my world won't change one bit if I don't have them. I have possessions I can play with at will, a food budget that graciously appears every month, and a warm bed to sleep in every night. I'm blessed with good health, as are my husband and children. I have a relationship with God and the power of the Holy Spirit to keep me connected to Him as I roam about this life.

It doesn't really matter how much I have, or how little. The important thing is, no matter what my portion, it is all a gift from God—freely given for my enjoyment, carefully crafted to meet my needs.

Still, I envy my dog's contentment.

Stella is blissfully unaware that any other life exists beyond what I've provided. I don't want her to feel pampered; I want her to feel safe. She doesn't need to be indulged; she needs to be loved. I don't meet her demands; I anticipate her needs. Stella has exactly what I want her to have—no more, no less. Outside of woeful disobedience and destructive behavior she can do nothing to change that. Oh, she can nuzzle her way through the Saran Wrap and finish off the Christmas pumpkin pie, or she can snatch the last piece of pizza languishing in the box on the table, but neither of these attempts to add to her cup will give her what she really wants.

My pleasure. My blessing.

These forays don't afford the pleasure she gets when she's called into the kitchen in the morning for an unexpected slice of cheese while I'm making the boys' lunches. But even then, when I've called her into my presence, when I have a feast (well, cheese) prepared to lay at her table, I'll impose the limits only a master can set. I'll hold it out in an open hand and say, "Leave it!" until I'm certain she could walk away, unfulfilled.

Then I make sure she doesn't.

6

Everything's Better with Cheddar

"Take It!"

But you would be fed with the finest of wheat;
with honey from the rock I would satisfy you.

PSALM 81:16

*H*alf a slice of meatloaf drizzled with ketchup, three little lumps of mashed potatoes, approximately nine green beans, two slices of yellow squash, and the bottom of a buttered roll—the remnants of a successful family dinner.

Yum.

As the rest of the family scatters to their evening retreats, I put the finishing touches on the plate of remnants, adding the crumbly bits from the meatloaf pan and pouring the last of the gravy over all of it.

Through the french doors that look out onto the patio, I can see Stella in exactly the same spot where she's been since I ushered her outside nearly an hour ago. She's no longer trying to assume any facade of dignity. Her ears are back, her eyes are wide; she sits tall, practically prancing in place. I can hear her high-pitched whines all the way in the kitchen.

On the floor next to the tall, blue plastic trash can sits a white dish full of untouched dog kibble and, next to it, the food dish of Clancie-the-cat. Knowing Stella is watching my every move, I set the plate—one of the pretty southwestern-style ones we got as a wedding gift—right down next to them. In between them, in fact.

Then I let her in.

Stella shoots through the door like a shiny black projectile, and I'm ready to indulge in our favorite behavior of all. It's the opposite of "Drop It!" The backside of "Leave It!" I get to lay out a feast for my beloved and tell her to "Take It!"

When Ramon takes us through the "Take It!" behavior, he paints an idealistic tableau of man and dog far beyond the scope of Intermediate Obedience. It's not enough that we'll be able to teach our dogs to "Leave It!" when they come across a pile of fresh poo on the sidewalk, or to "Drop It!" when they are entranced by the shininess of a new patent leather pump. Now we're supposed to be able to sit back in our La-Z-Boys, gesture toward some random object, and say, "Take It!" at which time our best friend will deliver said object cradled in a soft mouth. This is the image of the faithful companion fetching the newspaper in the icy predawn morning or greeting you at the door with soft slippers for your tired feet.

Ramon takes great pride telling us how Reese—his golden retriever with supercanine powers—will pick up and transport the remote control on command. I'm sure he's being modest, though. From what I've seen of Reese, he can probably pick up the remote, change the input from cable to video, pop in a DVD, and find the secret path-

> *I get to lay out a feast for my beloved and tell her to "Take it!"*

way past the commercials and previews straight to the main menu.

But the rest of us? I don't think so. Bitsy, the broken-tailed dachshund, seems so unaware of her surroundings she might not know what to take if you placed it in her mouth. Prima and Donna, the perpetually spinning yorkies, seem much more likely to "Take It!" and "Rip It!" to shreds between them. Of course there's always hope for Blanca, the three-month-old lab puppy, although right now she seems more likely to "Take It!" and it! and it! and...oooh...it! And Rex, the cool Australian shepherd mix—hey, Rex don't "Take It!" until Rex decides to "Take It!" Dig?

I don't like to link this particular behavior with any re-sponsibility on Stella's part. Rather, this is a time for me to lav-ish. To command her to enjoy a part of the life I'm giving her.

Sometimes it's a delicacy, like a plate full of supper served straight from my table, directly on my plate. Other times it's a simple, unexpected treat.

Every weekday morning at six thirty I can be found in the kitchen making lunches for my boys. Occasionally I mix it up with a foil-wrapped slice of leftover pizza or a meatball and mozzarella Hot Pocket, but most days it's the standby sandwiches. Peanut butter and jelly for Ryan; ham and cheese for Jack; ketchup and cheese for Charlie. Stella can be sound asleep on the foot of Jack's bed, but the minute I slide open that baggie of cheese, she's in the kitchen. It's actually kind of creepy. She's not there, I open the bag, I turn around, and there she is. Sometimes alert and ready, other times still in sleepy midstretch. She's here for one reason: she knows I'm going to peel off a piece of cheese, and she knows she's going to get to "Take It!"

Then I realize I'm not the only one ready to give that command, because Stella hasn't come in empty hand—er, paw—er, mouthed. She's brought in Cheeto, her favorite orange, formerly stuffed chew toy, and now it sits at my feet. She's not paying for cheese; she's not trading for cheese. She knows she's going to get this treat. So why the Cheeto-for-cheese moment?

Because she loves me.

Stella is the giver the Scriptures encourage: "Each man should give what he has decided in his heart to give, not reluctantly or under compulsion, for God loves a cheerful giver" (2 Corinthians 9:7). She has dropped Cheeto and now looks up at me with her tongue hanging out of her panting, grinning mouth. I was fully intending to give her cheese, but now I *want* to. I want to open the bag and peel off slice after slice. And maybe some ham too. Or a spoonful of peanut butter, just to see if she wants it. My sons are going to take their sack lunches and dutifully put them in their backpacks. Sure, they'll probably warm my heart with a "thanks" at some point (or not...), but they aren't here at my feet, handing over their Game Boy or cell phone. Cheeto may literally be a shell of what it once was, and I have absolutely no use for it, but I know what it means to Stella. For all she knows, I'm going to pick up that little orange scrap and throw it away, but instead I leave it for her enjoyment and heap cheddar blessings upon it.

Mike says I spoil my dog. And he's right. I love to love her, love to lavish her with treats. I keep a jar of biscuits at the door, and she gets one whenever she comes in. First thing— usually before the door closes behind her. But even there it's a mutual exchange. She always brings something inside—a leaf, a twig, a scrap from the chain-saw box she destroyed a few months ago. At first it irritated me, because I only saw a dog bringing in trash from outside. But now I see it for what it is. An offering.

Perhaps it came from her "Drop It!" training, where she was rewarded whenever she dropped anything from her mouth. But we've progressed way beyond that. Yes, it's a token—there's a whole big yard she could haul in, and if I kept every bit of it I'd probably have half of the backyard in my family room. But Stella delivers it with the expectation of a blessing. She's not hoarding the rest of the dirt clods and broken branches just in case she needs them later. Whatever she brings is a gift of her whole heart. She sees no difference between a dirt-encrusted rock and her beloved Cheeto. Or Squirrel (stuffed, not a real squirrel) or Purple Squeaky Man (not a real man). To her, everything's a treasure, and with abandon she says, "Take It!" And I hold out a treat—a biscuit or a dinner morsel or my cereal milk—and say, "Take It!"

> *Whatever she brings is a gift of her whole heart.*

Imagine such mutual giving with God. Giving Him as much as I can while He gives me as much as He wants. Especially knowing how much He wants to give me.

And what do I do? Well, let's just say that Jesus speaks directly to me:

"So do not worry, saying, 'What shall we eat?' or 'What shall we drink?' or 'What shall we wear?' For the pagans run after all these things, and your heavenly Father knows that you need them" (Matthew 6:31–32). That's right. Call me pagan. Because I spend an inordinate amount of time worrying. Sometimes, literally, about what I'll eat and drink. God has always graciously met those basic needs, but there's always that nagging fear. What if, at the end of the week, the end of the month, there's not enough? What if I write a check to my church, and twenty days later I'm trying to make a family dinner out of frozen, black bananas and the package of Thai noodles I found hiding behind the Bisquick? And I worry about what I'll wear—that I appear frumpy when I need to be chic; that everything I own screams, "Somebody please rescue this woman from her closet!"

I worry about my time, my talent, my energy. I look at the number of hours in my week, the number of things I need to accomplish, and I want to give up. So instead of plunging headfirst into doing what God wants, giving what He desires, going where He directs, I cower in a corner with a pint of Starbuck's Coffee Almond Fudge ice cream. A bad choice all around because at $4.95, we really can't afford it. And at eight hundred calories, it ensures that I'm too bloated to wear my cute capris to the church's community outreach event that I don't plan to attend anyway. I keep the insignificant scraps of myself piled up in my yard, offering Him nothing.

Here's where Stella definitely out-Christians me. Jesus says, "But seek first his kingdom and his righteousness, and all these things will be given to you as well" (Matthew 6:33). I don't always seek Jesus first—yet I sometimes expect my Master to give to me just the same. Just because.

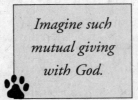

Imagine such mutual giving with God.

But Stella? She knows that no blessing, no treat, no reward ever comes without entering into my presence. And I am always there—ready with a blessing. Always prepared to meet her needs.

Cheese for Cheeto. Cheeto for cheese.

7

Cats and Frogs and Big, Barky Dogs

"Let's Go!"

Do two walk together unless they have agreed
to do so?

AMOS 3:3

*I*t's just after sundown. The dinner table has been cleared; the dishwasher hums in the background. My boys are finishing their homework, taking showers, getting their clothes ready for tomorrow. I notice something family friendly on television—most likely an Animal Planet documentary on the world's most carnivorous spiders, and the phone is ringing for the third time this hour.

Stella snoozes in the midst of the activity, curled on the couch with her nose tucked to her nub…until somebody says the magic phrase.

"Hey, Stella! Do you want to go for a walk?"

This is what it all sounds like to Stella:

Ifanybodyhasanydishesintheirroomtheyneedtobringthemtothekitchen becauseI'mabouttoturnonthedishwashersogocheckandsee.Momcould youlookovermyessaybeforeIturnitinbecauselasttimeIgota72andshesaidIneeded toproofread. TheblackcrestedGalapagosspiderconsumeshisownbodyweight duringthecourseofasingleweek. Momdidyouwashmybandshirtbecausewehaveto wearthemtomorrow. Ring! Ring! Somebodygetthephoneandifit'ssalesjusthangup. Seriously,gocheckyourroomfordishes. ShesaidIhadtoomanyrunonsentences. Hey Stella *doyouwanttogofora* walk?

Immediately her head pops up. She jumps off the couch, then sits pretty by the coat closet where we hang her leash. I've tried to condition my family to never utter this phrase unless somebody is ready, leash in hand, to take her for the afore-mentioned excursion, because once Stella hears the word, she's good to go. If we're not ready, she'll bounce between the leash and alternating family members—like an impatient four-legged pinball—until one of us gives in.

And of course, by one, I mean me.

"Remember," Ramon tells the class one Saturday, "*you* walk the *dog.* Not the other way around."

Apparently he's been spying on Stella and me when we're on our neighborhood outings. But I'm sure everybody here has some walking challenges. I've yet to see little broken-tail Bitsy take more than seven consecutive steps, while Blanca, the lab puppy, engages in something akin to gymnastics when she's at the end of a leash. Prima and Donna probably have a small doggie treadmill in their house so they don't have to risk getting their precious paws dirty. And I'm sure Rex triggers some supernatural Bruce Springsteen soundtrack whenever he takes a walk.

Despite her intrinsic cowardice, Stella, like any dog, has a willful, independent nature. Every moment on the far side of the front door is an adventure into a wide world, and she likes to snap up every bit of it.

Learning how to walk with her properly calls for some frustrating first steps. In fact, the first few steps aren't really steps at all. I lead Stella on her leash to an aisle in the store—this week I've chosen bird supplies. Before we can go any-where, I need to call Stella to my side and wait for her to sit at my feet. Then I make a little noise—something between a click and a kiss—and say, "Let's go!" We step out together, our tempos perfectly matched.

> *Despite her intrinsic cowardice, Stella, like any dog, has a willful, independent nature.*

But not for long.

Soon after hearing the word *go,* Stella picks up the speed, trotting out at a choke-neck pace. But, again, not for long. Once the leash is taut, I stop. She can strain as much as she wants, but she's not going anywhere. I call her back to my side; she sits; I give the command; we start again. Three white tile squares. She strains. I stop. She comes back. We can't even get down a birdseed aisle. How are we ever going to make it around the block?

Sure enough, as soon as we get home—even up to this day—almost every walk starts out this way, and it might keep up for nearly half a block. But then she realizes that I am her master, and she is my joy. Strolling through the neighborhood might be one of the great pleasures of her life, but if she's going to walk at all, she's going to have to walk beside me.

It's lovely once we find our groove. I get into a good cardio zone; she moves fast enough to keep herself interested. And what interests her most? Frogs.

After a big rain, our neighborhood becomes the second plague. Sometimes they are right there—little green globs in the middle of the sidewalk. More often they sit in the lawns as we stride by, blending in with the grass, with just the shiny glint of their slimy skin giving them away. As far as Stella is concerned, these squishy amphibians are the true treasure of Egypt. Left to her own devices, the creatures would be snatched right up—their little legs dangling from her dainty jaw. She does this not out of maliciousness or hunger, but pure entertainment.

Stella is like the Teacher in the book of Ecclesiastes who

says, "Come now, I will test you with pleasure to find out what is good" (2:1). Apparently her first chomp of a frog was good. But I, her master, find them abhorrent. Why, when she has Cheeto and Purple Squeaky Man and Squirrel—not to mention a houseful of socks at her disposal—would she feel a need to dabble in this disgusting pursuit? So, when Stella's snout starts to seek out that frog, I'm quick to give her the, "Uh, uh. Leave it!" For good measure, she might get a little jerk of the leash too. Then, within the next few steps, just as the Teacher learns that the pursuit of pleasure is meaningless, the enticing amphibian is forgotten.

In the same way the occasional frog inspires a momentary jolt of cheerful rebellion, the certainty of big, barking dogs is a source of constant fear. In her heart, Stella is insecure. Protected by the solid planks of our backyard fence, she can patrol her territory, woofing it up like a guard monster in a pink sparkling collar. But out in the neighborhood, with only a leash to offer protection, she tends to be much more wary.

By now I know which houses have the big, barky dogs, so I steer us clear of them as much as possible. Sometimes, though, one will unexpectedly run up behind its fence or will be out patrolling its own front yard, and I can feel Stella tense every muscle through the leash. Her hackles rise up, and I know she's scared. She doesn't bark back like she would at home. She stops, trembles, and tries to back away.

That's when my heart breaks. I hate the thought of Stella being afraid. I would never want her to think that I would lead her into danger or that I would stop at anything to keep her safe.

The Lord constantly reassures me of my safety in Him. But still, how often do I tremble at the end of my leash? Sometimes it's hard to buy into the fact that God did not give me a "spirit of timidity" (2 Timothy 1:7), because there are so many things to be afraid of. Death, debt, and disease bark behind invisible fences—hidden for now, but ready to pounce. I could be strolling happily through life, enjoying the flowers and sidestepping the frogs, and *bark-bark-boom*! Whatever flimsy fence had been keeping me safe could fall, and there I'd be. Exposed.

One day a few years ago, in the midst of coaching our twins' baseball team, Mike discovered he couldn't throw the ball. Weeks went by, and he started to drop things. One minute he'd be holding a glass of water, and the next minute—*boom*. On the floor. Then stranger things started to happen. Uncontrollable tremors in his left hand. Then his leg. One day I traced a big *thump* noise down the hall and found him on the floor. He hadn't tripped; he just fell. We couldn't ignore the problem anymore. I looked down and said, "Hey, Mikey! Wanna go to the doctor?"

Our walk through the neighborhood of diagnosis was one of the longest of my life. Mikey and I went from doctor to doctor, through x-rays and MRIs, blood work, and CT scans. Each possibility barked a different threat. Multiple sclerosis? Lou Gehrig's disease? For months we lived with our individual fears. I was terrified at the thought of losing my husband, and

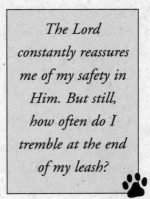

The Lord constantly reassures me of my safety in Him. But still, how often do I tremble at the end of my leash?

Mike was terrified at the thought of depending on me for long-term care.

"Seriously, Al," he said on the drive back from a round of tests, "if it's something really bad, promise me you'll drop me off at the nearest nursing home."

As unavoidable as those scary times were, they would have seemed unconquerable if either Mike or I had roamed through them alone. But we didn't. We had each other; more than that, we were leashed to God. Thankfully, He steered us away from any debilitating dangers as we discovered that Mikey had a spinal stenosis—a narrowing of the nerve openings around the spinal cord. Completely correctable, and something that would have seemed much worse if we hadn't just escaped from the jaws of a more serious illness. After a six-hour surgery, twelve titanium screws, a five-inch titanium plate, a sprinkling of cadaver vertebrae, and three months in a neck brace, Mikey is now fine. Walking without falling, not dropping the leash.

Stella and I take a route around the neighborhood that requires us to double back on three streets before reaching the final loop that leads us home. Often (and I mean four out of five walks) that final curve reveals a huge white cat that lounges right in the middle of a sidewalk square from which he refuses to move—ever—despite the oncoming threat of a forty-pound dog and her power-walking master. Most cats bring out Stella's playful side; she might take a few ear-perked bounding steps in their general direction, but whenever we come upon *this* cat, Stella stops—five sidewalk squares away.

I praise Stella for sitting pretty, then give the click-kiss sound and tell her to walk with me again. Which she does—for one more square. She stops. I praise, click-kiss, and walk. She follows. One square. She stops. Meanwhile, the cat, to his credit, doesn't move. Doesn't arch his back or hiss. He simply swishes his tail back and forth and stares. When we're only one square away from the cat, Stella stops again—this time, she's behind me. No amount of click-kisses or walk commands will budge her. So, I change her course, lead her out into the street, avoiding the cat, and away we stroll.

It's such a frustrating, unreasonable fear. Anybody who's ever watched a cartoon knows that dog trumps cat. Stella, in her stubbornness and insecurity, refuses to acknowledge superiority to her enemy. I wish she could see that the two of us, through the power of our leash, could walk right across that cat without getting a scratch. We could stomp on top of the feline if we wanted to. Each time we come across it, I think, *Maybe this will be the time that Stella walks across the cat.*

Our detour doesn't make me love her any less; I just hate that she's missing out on the satisfaction of triumphing over an enemy.

One night we encounter the cat twice. Once, in front of what must be his house, then again as we walk up the opposite side of the street. (Yes, the cat crossed the street; I think I heard violins playing the theme from

> *Anybody who's ever watched a cartoon knows that dog trumps cat.*

Psycho somewhere in the distance.) This time, however, the cat isn't on just any old square. He's lounging on a strip of sidewalk that creates a bridge over a drainage ditch with a barrier fence erected on either side.

Stella and I begin our white cat dance. Stop, click-kiss, one square, sit. Stop, click-kiss, one square, sit. By the time we get to Stella's point of no return, we're on the bridge—no street for a detour. Thinking this might be Stella's day, I take one step over the cat. Stella doesn't move. I take another; Stella stays still. The leash stretches out between us. When I turn around to face her, she's sitting pretty—panting a little—with the white cat motionless between us and the leash pulled taut.

"Come on, Stella," I say. "Walk on over that cat. You can do it."

If we were living in the final minutes of a Disney movie, music would swell in the background as she stands tall and prances right over the cat, who would be forced to jump into the drainage ditch below. But this is life—life with Stella—and she simply stares. The cat shifts his gaze from me to Stella and back again. I could yank the leash or kick the cat. But I don't. I step back over—to Stella's side—and lead her off the bridge, into the street, then onto the sidewalk again. Walking past the cat—or *over* the cat—is a blessing she may never know, but at least we're still walking together.

Two and a half miles later, one ribbon-like loop around

the neighborhood, our house is in sight, just three doors up. Stella is exhausted by this time. It's hard to believe that the slow-moving, panting, pretty girl at the end of the leash is the same feisty creature who, just an hour ago, lunged off the sidewalk chasing some phantom scent. By now, the leash is figurative. I keep it loosely looped over my pinkie. At this point, not even the biggest, friskiest frog could tempt Stella off her course.

Home is near.

For Stella, the reward is a bowl of fresh water (or an open toilet seat), maybe a slice of cheese if the kids are packing their lunches for tomorrow. On hot July nights, we know we'll be hit by a blast of refrigerated air; in frigid February the house will be warm and welcoming. I talk to Stella a lot during these final steps, praising her for being such a good walker, telling her what a pretty girl she is. Prettier than she has been on any part of our evening's journey. When we come to our own front porch, I stop and call Stella to sit at my feet. I reach down and unhook the leash before opening the front door. Still sitting, she looks up at me and waits for the final command.

"Go!" I tell her, and we walk inside—together.

8

Praise for the Invisible Dog

"Come!"

I will heal their waywardness
and love them freely,
for my anger has turned away from them.

HOSEA 14:4

When Stella runs, she looks like a sleek black ribbon sprung from a spool. When she comes in through the back door, her nails make little *rip-rip* sounds as she shreds a microscopic path from the door, twice around the couch, then back to sit and wait for a treat. When she's let out into the backyard, her paws kick up small dirt clods as she tears down the real path she's worn through the grass, to the back fence, twice around the tree, then back to the door where she sits and waits to come back inside. And get a treat.

If she's in the front yard, though, it's a straight path to gonesville. If I squint and try to focus within the blur, I can see her in midair, all four paws off the ground. Like momentary bursts of flying. While it's a beautiful sight to behold, it's a terrifying one as well, especially when those four flying feet are taking her away.

The world's a scary place for a running dog.

In week four of Intermediate Obedience, Ramon asks, "Does your dog come to you when you call its name?"

Here is something we all have in common. Of course our dogs don't come when we call them. That would be obedience, and we're all here because our dogs won't obey. Blanca is far too caught up in her frantic, fuzzy, puppy world to even know her name. Prima and Donna are so infatuated with each other, they present a united front of disdain for whatever mere mortal would dare to summon them. Now, broken-tail Bitsy has so far exhibited the personality of a Wheat Thin, so her lack of response isn't so much rebellion as it is extended processing time. But Rex? With that red bandanna around his neck? Let him off the leash in an open space, and baby, he was born to run.

Stella has a three-step response to the calling of her name. First, she freezes. Second, she piddles. Third, she runs—in the opposite direction.

There was a time when our family had to build fifteen minutes into any departure in order to allow time for rounding up Stella. Whether we were going to church, to a movie, out to dinner, or to a ball game, the final detail before leaving the house was to herd Stella out to the backyard. Leaving her in the house was out of the question ever since an unfortunate incident with the bookcase.

Stella would take to hiding under one of the boys' beds the minute she sensed that we were leaving, so we'd trained ourselves to walk around the house slowly, speaking in low, even tones, and hiding behind closed doors to put on shoes and jackets. Sometimes that worked, and we'd catch her by surprise as she napped on the family room couch. From there it was a simple matter of assigning someone to block the hallway while somebody else stood on the back porch, treat in hand, luring the unsuspecting girl out the back door. But more often, Stella would pick up on the impending desertion and high-nub it to the back of the house to take her chances in the underbelly of a teenager's room.

Then it would be time for the family to work together. Ryan was charged with coaxing Stella out from under the bed—inch by inch—while my youngest boy, Charlie, crept up and down the hall shutting all the other bedroom doors. Meanwhile, Ryan's twin, Jack, took his place at the front of the hallway, ready to coax Stella on the second leg of the journey. I would be stationed at the back door, trying to look nonchalant.

The house would ring with the sound of calling, "Stella!" *"Stella!" "STELLA!"* "Stella!" Slowly she'd emerge from under the bed, then meander out of the room, then slink down the hall into the family room. So close. So very, very close. Unfortunately, sometimes I made the rookie mistake of not having the back door open, and the minute my hand hit the door-knob, Stella would panic and squat. That's usually the time Mikey would come in from waiting in the car and, in his six-foot-tall voice, demand to know just what the problem was. That was Stella's chance to make a break for it; she'd spin and take off back down the hall. According to the muffled *thump,* Ryan had done his part by closing the door. But our job would be harder, because now she knew. Oh, she sus-pected before, but now she was certain. We weren't calling her out of the kindness of our hearts; we were calling her to kick her out.

Does our faithful canine come when we call her name? In a word, no.

In Intermediate Obedience we learn that the key to get-ting your dog to respond is to always, always call your dog using a tone of voice dripping with welcoming joy. And you have to mean it, really, because a dog can smell insincerity. You need to summon your dog with a lilt of love—even if she's halfway down the block and you're outside in a towel; even if she's tearing through the park with a sandwich stolen from your picnic; even if she's huddling under a bed and you're about to be late for church. Again. In any case, the most important thing is that your dog obeys your voice. That she return to you. And if that is the main objective, it's your job to ensure a happy reunion. After all, dogs aren't stupid. If given a choice, who would willingly return to an irate master?

We have a fabulous disc golf course in a park near our home. Stella gets excited the moment she sees Mike and the boys pull their disc bags out of the closet because she knows exactly what that means—hours and hours of romping, running fun. (I'll go along, too, but only for the experience of walking in the park; I stink at the actual game.)

According to Mike, the object of the game is to throw the disc into the basket. According to Stella, the object is to chase down the disc and do with it what she pleases. But Mikey has come up with a solution. He brings a purple disc specifically for Stella. Now, this is not an official disc golf disc. It's just a cheap flying toy, completely unsuitable for play-

> *Always call your dog using a tone of voice dripping with welcoming joy. And you have to mean it, really, because a dog can smell insincerity.*

ing the game—kind of like a gumball on a regular golf course. Before setting himself up for his throw, Mike flings the purple disc away from the target. It's a total distraction tactic, and it works every time. Stella's off like a shot, running full-out free in the park, oblivious to the real game going on behind her back. Her long red leash trails behind her; acres and acres of grass and trees are at her disposal. She's running for the sake of running, the purple disc little more than an excuse.

This is when I begin to get worried. Stella's about as far away from me as she can get in the park, and she's not interested in fetching the purple disc *back* to me, because she hasn't mastered the finer points of fetch. In fact, not even the most obvious point of fetch. If she comes back, it's only because I call her to me. So I do.

"Stella!" My voice rings out. She stops cold and perks up her ears.

"Stella!" She starts to run back and then... *Oops! The disc.* She turns away from me, circles around, hunts it down, then scoops it up within her jaws.

I call and I call, my voice full of love and platitudes. She's my bella. My darling. My sweet puppy. Anybody within the sound of my voice knows how much I love this dog. She knows it too. From a distance I can see her bounding toward me, and my heart always races a bit when she's close enough that I can look right into her dark brown eyes. That's when her path seems to straighten. It's as if the closer she gets, the faster she runs. Then, always, when she's about five yards away, *ptooey*! She spits out that disc. Drops the very thing that sent her away and circles around me once, twice. And when I tell her to sit, she comes to a shuddering halt—vibrating like a plucked guitar string. It takes quite a bit of coaxing to get her to go back, get the disc, and drop it at my feet, but she eventually will.

Then we start all over again.

I was a senior in high school when the world threw a purple disc for me. Up until that point, I was every Christian, church-going, Lord-loving family's daughter—in church every time the doors were open, hanging out in the parking lot when they weren't. My world was my youth group. Pick any slogan on any Christian T-shirt, and that was my life. No drinks, no drugs. No smokes, no sex. I was the girl who'd rather be chaste than chased. For seventeen years I'd been content living out my days as a simple walk in the park with my family. Then, fling! Up in the sky there was this bright, colorful, spinning orb, and I was off like a shot, running full out.

Anybody within the sound of my voice knows how much I love this dog.

But not free. You're never really free when you're running from God.

What was I chasing? The allure of the college keg-fueled party. The boyfriend who played in a rock band, the boyfriend with the black belt in karate, the boyfriend who spoke French. The really, really smart guy who just didn't love me. Countless dangerous decisions. An abundance of deceit.

I was head down, ears flat, running as fast and as far as I could, right into a vast spiritual desert, as stiff-necked and stubborn as anybody determined to run away from God. But just as God spoke to His wayward people thousands of years ago, He spoke to me: "People of Israel, return to the LORD, the God of Abraham, Isaac and Israel, that he may return to you" (2 Chronicles 30:6). Not an angry, "Get back here *now!*" Not an accusatory, "Look what you've *done!*" Not a threatening, "Wait'll I get my *hands* on you!" Rather, like the proclamation that was sent throughout the realm of Israel and Judah, the command is full of encouraging promise "Return to the LORD...submit to the LORD. Come to the sanctuary...Serve the LORD"—ending with this assurance—"The LORD your God is gracious and compassionate. He will not turn his face from you if you return to him" (2 Chronicles 30:7–9).

I could always hear God calling me, and I did turn back occasionally. But never completely. Never for long. I was terrified of repentance. I didn't want to face what I'd become. The longer I kept running, the easier it was for me to keep my shame at bay. I could convince myself that my life was just fine. That I wasn't hurting anyone. That I was living a life of pure, unadulterated joy.

But after a while I had to stop. And when I did, I was faced with two alternatives. I could turn around, or I could stay stuck. By this point, I'd grown up. I'd collided with Mike who was running away too, though not nearly as fast and furious as I was. We'd moved away from our college town where ghosts of bad decisions lurked behind every darkened door. We were going to church almost as often as we weren't; we were living a good, (mostly) clean life, posing no immediate harm to ourselves or others.

But it wasn't enough. People often say that, just before coming to know the Lord, they realize that there was "something missing" in their lives. I never really felt like *God* was missing from *my* life—because I'd never completely abandoned my faith. My belief. My deep-down love for my Savior. What I felt was much worse. I felt like *God* was missing *me*. Like I'd lost my place

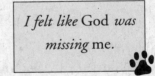

I felt like God *was missing* me.

with Him. And one night, at the close of a session at a Christian writers conference, I was determined to get it back.

Despite years of hearing about the wonders of God's grace, I still anticipated a moment of awkwardness between my repentance and God's forgiveness. I saw myself standing next to my pile of sin, shifting on my spiritual feet, waiting for the final verdict. But when I finally turned around and ran home, I discovered something wonderful.

God's forgiveness was already there, waiting for me to take it.

Back in class, Ramon teaches us all a sure-fire trick to get any running dog to turn around.

"If your dog won't come back to you, just kneel down and praise the invisible dog that does."

We all give him quizzical looks, so he demonstrates. Right there in the middle of the baby-gate circle at the back of the pet store, Ramon gets down on one knee and—odd as it sounds—praises an invisible dog. He lowers his head to make invisible eye contact and says, "Good dog! Good boy!" while positioning his hand to scratch behind invisible ears. He even gets carried away and plants a kiss on an invisible nose. And an amazing thing happens: every dog in the circle is immediately drawn to the display. Stella, who had just moments ago been trying to wedge her way behind the hedge of protection known as my legs, is suddenly dying to get over to Ramon to see what the fuss is all about. I want to chalk it up to the fact that Ramon's making the same kissy-kiss sound that I do to praise her, but there's something more.

Later that week I forget to make the requisite I'm-coming-home-from-the-grocery-store-make-sure-Stella's-outside phone call. When I get home, I struggle through the front door with my arms full of groceries, and Stella barrels right past me. Like always, she makes a straight shot to the corner of the yard, gives a quick glance back, then she's off again. I call the boys out and we position ouselves—one across the street, one blocking the alley, one three houses down in the opposite direction. And I stay right by the front door and call.

"Stella!"

There's a stronger spirit of rebellion in her this day—or else she'd simply been cooped up for too long—because there's no coercing her to come back. She stops and turns around, but the minute any of us makes the slightest move toward her, she's gone again.

Then, like an intermediate Jedi, I hear Ramon's voice.

"Praise the invisible dog."

I decide not to take another step. I won't chase her. I shouldn't have to. Instead, right there in the middle of my front yard, I get down on one knee, hold my hands out, and say, "Good girl!" I speak loud enough that she can hear me, but not loud enough to sound like calling. She stops, four houses down, and turns around.

"Pretty girl!" I say, running my hands down an invisible black back. "What a pretty, pretty girl!"

Stella takes a few steps toward me.

"Come on! Come on!" I pat my legs—not in the grand gesture I'd use to call a dog back from four houses down, but little pats, the ones I'd use to call her just a little closer. Like when she's sitting right in front of me and I want her to give me a kiss. Or when she's at my feet and I'm inviting her to sit right next to me. Then I pretend she *is* right there, her front paws on my legs, and I lean back, laughing.

"Oh, what a funny, good girl!" I'm pretending to ruffle imaginary brown ears, then to scratch that soft spot just below a nonexistent white-spotted throat—her favorite spot. Who could resist such love? Who wouldn't want such lavish attention? What could those unfamiliar houses peopled with strangers possibly offer that would be greater than this?

The next thing I know, my girl is running. As fast as she can. Straight to me. Fitting perfectly into the Stella-sized embrace I've prepared for her.

9

Patience Is Averting

"Wait!"

Yet the LORD longs to be gracious to you;
  he rises to show you compassion.
For the LORD is a God of justice.
  Blessed are all who wait for him!

ISAIAH 30:18

*S*tella is one happy girl. It's a crisp fall day, and the entire backyard is a blanket of soft fallen leaves. A few months ago, during our rainy season, we bought a mat to act as a mud-catcher at the back door. As usual—and to Mikey's unfailing irritation—Stella has dragged it away from its proper place on the porch to make a little nest for herself under the Arizona ash tree. In the afternoon, a perfect triangle of bright sunlight forms right at the base of its trunk. Stella's there now, stretched out on the purloined mat. In a gesture of divine contentment, she rolls onto her back—her paws scooping up a few scattered leaves as she turns. Soon her white-speckled breast and soft pink tummy bask in the warmth of the autumn day. Her eyes are closed tight, and I'm envious of her nap.

I've actually come to the back door intending to call her in, but the scene is so peaceful, so serene, I can't imagine disturbing it. As I turn away, however, my hand brushes against the door-knob, bringing an end to the tranquillity. The sound of that tiny rattle speeds across the yard and *boing*! Stella's eyes pop open, her head turns, and she becomes a frantic, twisting mess trying to right herself to her feet. Leaves scatter everywhere as she scrambles, and they fly out in the wake of her paws as she tears toward the door. Because if there's anything Stella likes more than being outside, it's coming back in.

As Stella runs pell-mell from her sunny Shangri-la, a few stray leaves cling to her coat, and I'm positive the race across her self-made path will mean tiny clumps of mud clinging to her paws. It's not that I don't want her to come inside, I just think maybe she should—*crash*! Before the door opens wide enough for her thin frame, she's somehow inside. *Crash* is the perfect word for it too. Stella's impatience often comes with the sound effect of the top of her skull colliding with the side of the door. I wince at the horrible cracking sound because it's my fault.

I forgot to tell her to wait.

In Intermediate Obedience, we learn that teaching a dog to "wait" is really the most sophisticated of all the commands. It's not like "sit" or "stay," where the dog is rooted in one po-sition—perhaps indefinitely. It's a command with an unspoken promise: "You'll get what you want, go where you want in a little while. For now, I just need you to…wait." It calls for the dog to recognize an unspoken, invisible barrier—one imposed only by the master's will. It's arbitrary, subtle, abstract, and conditional.

Frankly, Stella's not very good at it.

"Pretend this is the kitchen," Ramon says to us as we're gathered in the circle of baby gates. "You're busy cooking dinner, and you don't want your dog to come in."

Suddenly Reese, Ramon's freakishly obedient golden lab, appears at the baby-gate opening. I don't know exactly where he hangs out during the rest of the class time. I picture him lounging in the back of the store, wearing half-glasses and working the daily Sudoku until the clock on the break room wall tells him it's time to make his appearance. Now he's wandered up aisle seventeen and just about to walk in when Ramon moves over to stand in the gate opening.

> *It calls for the dog to recognize an unspoken, invisible barrier—one imposed only by the master's will.*

"Wait," he says to Reese. And Reese stops. He doesn't sit (he hasn't been told to sit); he doesn't lie down (he hasn't been given that command). He simply stops walking. "Now," Ramon says, turning his attention to his lower-achieving students, "he won't come past that point until I tell him to.

"Why not make him sit?" I ask, secretly wishing he would crash the gate.

"He doesn't need to sit," Ramon says. "He just can't cross this line."

"Why not tell him to stay?" I persist as Reese paces lazily to and fro on the other side.

"I don't need him to stay," Ramon says. "He can go and do anything he wants to, but he can't cross this threshold until I tell him to."

At this point Stella has crawled under and around my seat, effectively lashing my leg to the chair leg with her leash. We've barely mastered "Sit!" and "Stay!" is still a hit-and-miss. Getting her to wait politely? I don't see that happening any time soon. When Stella has her little doggy-mind set on something, she wants it. If she's outside, she wants inside.

Now, please.

If she's inside she wants outside. She calmly approaches as you're sitting on the couch, plants her paws on your knees, then walks them up to your chest, then stretches her nose close to yours, and gives the tiniest, high-pitched whine.

Outside? Now, please?

She paces around the dinner table, strains the leash when she walks, thoroughly pokes her nose into every package or bag that comes into the house. Once we brought home a new bookcase from Ikea—the land of boxed, bring-home, and build furniture—and left it on the living room floor, still in its package. Unfortunately, we also left Stella alone inside, and when we got home, the box was a pile of cardboard crumbs. I tried to defend her, telling Mikey that if we had left the box label side up, she wouldn't have felt the need to open it herself to see what was inside. He did not agree.

Since she'll never learn to read, she'll have to learn to wait.

"To teach this at home," Ramon says, "take your dog someplace where there's a narrow doorway. Then, stand with him on one side, say, 'Wait,' then back out through the door. If the dog tries to follow you, block the doorway with your body."

"Block it how?" I ask, coaxing Stella out from underneath my chair.

"With your body," he says. "With your legs. Just don't let the dog get past you."

Ah.

I look around at Stella's fellow students. Bitsy seems too dull to pass through a doorway. Prima and Donna are probably carried from room to room. Blanca stands as much a chance of waiting at the door as I do of winning the next Miss Teen New Jersey pageant. And Rex would probably just slip his master a fiver to see if there was any way we could get him through that door a little sooner, you know what I mean, Jack?

Ramon doesn't seem to understand that Stella is like liquid lightning when she wants to go somewhere. I could try to block her, but she's going to ooze right past me. I try to explain this, but he stops me in midsentence.

"Remember, you're the master. Stand at the door, and tell her to wait."

And then it comes to me. While I teach this behavior, it won't be my verbal command that wills Stella to obey, it will be my body. More than that, not my body, but my presence.

I had no idea how hard this was going to be, which is odd, because nobody has a harder time waiting than I do.

I'm the person who opens her mail at the mailbox and checks e-mail about every hour. I glare at people with eleven items in the express checkout line. Mike is always after me for not locking the car door, but I can't stand the extra fraction of a second it takes to *bwoop-bwoop* the button. My impatience is why I'm constantly leaving the house without the checkbook, getting to church without my Bible, looking in the mirror to see that I only have mascara on one eye. People talk about the patience of Job. I'm more like Mrs. Job: "Curse God and die!" That'd be my first response to the world of hurt that fell upon that family.

Come to think of it, I'd be equally as horrible as Mrs. Noah, watching my husband build this unheard-of monstrosity for a nebulous disaster. And then, once it was done? When we were loaded up with all the animals... Those seven days waiting for God to come around and close the door would have been downright unbearable.

And Rachel? I can't imagine waiting seven years to marry the man I love, only to wait another seven after he's accidentally paired up with my older, less attractive (if more fertile) sister. Had I been Rachel, I would have taken that hunk's hand and run off to an Old Testament equivalent of Las Vegas.

> *I had no idea how hard this was going to be, which is odd, because nobody has a harder time waiting than I do.*

I think about Hannah, all those years praying for a child. Begging God. Imploring her heavenly Father. What was at the core of all that heartfelt petition? Waiting...waiting and waiting and waiting. Yet Hannah did it with grace, without complaining, without tapping her foot and glaring at Little Miss Peninnah, her fellow wife with all the kids. And when

God gave Hannah a son? When He finally allowed her to come over the threshold into motherhood? She gave the boy right back to Him. The very thought of it makes me crazy.

A great scene at the end of *Star Wars: Episode I* shows the Jedi master Qui-Gon Jinn facing the final battle with the evil Sith, Darth Maul. They've displayed a masterful bit of fighting with their light sabers, and now it's time for the decisive exchange. Qui-Gon Jinn and the Sith find themselves on opposite sides of an electronic force field—an invisible wall keeping both of them from completing their missions. On one side, the peaceful Jedi master kneels, closes his eyes, and settles himself. On the other, Darth Maul paces, his black and red face a visage of evil. He brandishes his light saber, slicing through the air—impatient to confront his foe. Finally, the force field lifts, the two engage in a furious battle, and in a tragic twist, the forces of evil conquer the forces of good.

I have the patience of a Sith lord too often, and when I allow for an unsettling in my spirit, I know that's one battle that the dark side has won.

The only logical doorway to use to teach Stella to "Wait!" is the one that leads to the backyard. On our first attempt, I open the door, and Stella barrels between my legs before I can say the word. I round her up, lure her back outside with a treat, then start again. This time I open the door a couple of inches—just enough to get my lips through to say, "Wait." Then I open it a little more, saying, "Wait." And just a few inches more, filling the open space solid with my body.

"Wait."

The oddest thing happens. Stella sits down.

I crack the door another inch wider, and she stands up. But as she takes that first step toward the door, I repeat, "Wait."

She sits down again.

Another inch. She stands.

"Wait." Sit.

Another inch. Stand. By this time the door is open wide enough that she could easily slip past me into the house. But she doesn't. Oddly, she doesn't sit either. Instead, she turns and starts to move around in a nervous little circle. Whenever Stella is particularly anxious, she has a way of walking that turns her whole body into the shape of a parenthesis. She's doing that now, walking away from me and looking back at the same time. It's like she's asking, *Do you see me? I'm still right here. You're right there. So...*

Another inch. "Wait," I say, only this time I take a step away from the open door. Stella doesn't look at me. She doesn't sit, either. Instead, she widens the circumference of her circle and picks up a stick in her mouth, just to be ready.

Another couple of inches. Another step back. I take my hand completely off the doorknob and say nothing. It's a wide-open path inside, but still Stella waits. It isn't easy for her—she's a frazzled wreck, and I can tell it's in the back of her little mind to rush inside. But she doesn't. She's held at bay, not by my body or my voice, but by my presence.

It's a tense little time for both of us as we stare at each other. But to truly test the behavior, I have to step back. Turn away. Leave a completely invisible presence in the doorway. When I do, there's a visible change in Stella. She goes from being confused to nervous to genuinely hurt. She walks a slow, wide circle around the back porch and whines. If she could speak, she might quote the words of the psalm: "Do not hide your face from me, do not turn your servant away in anger; you have been my helper. Do not reject me or forsake me, O God my Savior" (Psalm 27:9).

Stella can't understand why she should ever have to wait. She doesn't see the problem with muddy paws that need to be wiped. She doesn't realize the danger and temptation of the open front door. She can't imagine why she should have to wait for the leftovers to be scraped onto one plate—all the little bits of meat and gravy that I gather just for her. All she knows is that this body—this voice—no, this *presence* keeps her at a perpetual threshold.

God keeps me waiting for all the same reasons. Sometimes I need to be groomed—cleansed through repentance and study before I'm allowed to take on a new challenge. Sometimes I'm not able to see the dangers lurking around the corners

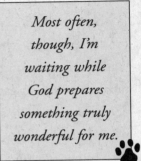

Most often, though, I'm waiting while God prepares something truly wonderful for me.

of life; in fact, sometimes I can't even see the corners. Most often, though, I'm waiting while God prepares something truly wonderful for me. Lining up my husband. Preparing me to have children. Perfecting the time for me to change careers.

That doesn't make it any easier though. In those times when I wait on the porch, when God has the door wide open while He's willing me to wait, I need to remember the words of hope that conclude the psalm:

I am still confident of this:
    I will see the goodness of the LORD
    in the land of the living.
Wait for the LORD;

be strong and take heart
and wait for the LORD.
(Psalm 27:13–14)

Now, when Stella wants to come inside, she waits when I tell her to, and she charges if I don't. And every now and then when it's a perfect sunny day—not too hot, not too cold, no rain, no wind—I leave her outside. She might whine at the door, but eventually she'll remember the beauty of the world the true Master created, and she'll pick up her mat, drag it back to her tree, and lie down in the sunshine.

I figure she'll thank me for it later.

10

A Hefty Promise

"Watch Me!"

He will not let your foot slip—
    he who watches over you will not slumber;
indeed, he who watches over Israel
    will neither slumber nor sleep.

PSALM 121:3–4

The first sign of trouble is a pudding cup. It's empty. More than empty, really. Licked clean. And it sits where no self-respecting pudding cup should be—on the floor behind our huge, striped swivel chair. Not quite under the long table that displays all our family photographs. The foil lid lies a few feet away, fully detached, and the plastic spoon, now snapped in half. I begin to reconstruct the crime immediately. Oh, I could attribute it to a careless child, dropping his Snack Pack wherever he pleases. Goodness knows a pudding cup on the floor in any of their rooms would not be an unusual sight. But here, in the family room, behind the striped chair—there's only one explanation.

Then I spot the foam tray that once held a pound of extra-lean ground beef, and nearby, the empty envelope of taco seasoning. Scattered about are bits and pieces of credit card offers and timeshare advertisements. These have been cut with scissors with precise, straight lines, unlike the shredded potato chip bags and Rice-A-Roni box I discover on the kitchen floor. The scene makes the name "Hefty" a laughable one. Those superstrong expanding diamonds give no defense against the determined paws of a dog left alone, overnight, with a bag of trash.

At this very moment—6:35 on a Sunday morning—an unrepentant Stella trots in on those four determined paws.

Two minutes ago I was standing at the open doorway of my son Jack's room where Stella had been curled up asleep at the foot of his bed. She'd heard my approach, opened one big, brown eye. When I said, "Good morning, my pretty girlie-girl," she grunted a reply, stretched her long legs out until her claws scratched the wall, yawned until I was afraid her jaw would unhinge. Then she puts herself back together—mouth closed, four paws flat on the floor beneath her, ready for the morning romp outside.

One minute ago I was turning on the lamp by the bookcase, ready to make my way to the kitchen to warm up the oven for the pan of Sunday sausage kolaches. I was listening to Stella's tags jingling as she treated herself to a vigorous morning scratch. I was in the middle of a kiss-kiss call, telling my beloved to hurry up and go outside...

That's when I saw the pudding cup.

When Stella first steps into the living room, it's like any other morning—her ears are up. She prances a bit. Her eyes are clear and bright. When she looks up, I almost expect to hear Debbie Reynolds' voice sing out "Good mornin', good mooornin'..." as she trots by.

Except now I'm holding the pudding cup, and she immediately looks away.

"Stella?" I say in that long, drawn out way I use when I'm trying to wheedle a confession out of one of my children. Of course Stella doesn't confess. Aside from the fact that she can't, there's no need to when the evidence covers an eight-foot amorphous area between the kitchen and family room. Instead, she simply refuses to look at me. She bops right past me on her way to the backdoor, completely avoiding any acknowledgment of my presence.

"Stella, did you get in the trash?" It's a silly rhetorical question at best, but Stella reacts to it as if the words were a physical slap, backs two or three steps away from me, and stares at something apparently fascinating on the tip of my knees.

"Look at me, Stella," I say, bending low so that my face is inches away from hers. Normally this would elicit a quick lick on my nose or an affectionate nuzzle, but the chocolate-encrusted Exhibit A in my hand is like affection kryptonite, and Stella moves away to sit by the door, waiting patiently for me to open it. Under any other circumstances, this moment would be a hallmark of unspoken communication, with Stella looking at the doorknob, then at me, then at the doorknob again. But this morning she just sits quietly. Looking down. Her head isn't hanging in shame but moves with her shifting eyes, trying to find someplace safe to land.

Wherever she looks, there's a reminder of her disobedience. A Pop-Tart wrapper, an empty McDonald's cup, the lid from a quart of ice cream. To be truthful, though, it's not the evidence she's avoiding. After all, as far as random acts of canine crime are concerned, dogs have no memory. At this moment, hours after the act, Stella has no concept that she's done anything wrong. For me to chastise her or, even worse, punish her at this point would be useless and cruel. She's standing in the middle of a crime scene, and she doesn't have a clue. She only knows that I'm not happy.

> *As far as random acts of canine crime are concerned, dogs have no memory.*

For this reason, she cannot look me in the eye.

In Intermediate Obedience, we learned that the cornerstone to almost every desired behavior is making eye contact with the dog.

"The first thing you have to do," Ramon says, "is get your dog's attention. And the only way to know if you have your dog's attention is to know that your dog is looking at you." So all those Saturdays, whatever else I was teaching Stella to do, I was also teaching her to "Watch Me!" When I got her to sit, nub-down on the floor, I'd say, "Watch Me!" and our eyes would lock together.

"The second the dog looks away," Ramon says, "the dog is no longer being obedient."

So if Stella broke our gaze, I'd give her the ugly "Uh, uh" and startle her attention back to me.

"Watch me!" I'd say, and lavish praise the moment her big brown eyes met mine.

Practicing at home later, I'd tell Stella to "Sit!" or I'd get her "Down!" and without the extra command her eyes would meet mine. I felt like some kind of superhero, freezing her in place with the simple power of my gaze. I'd back away, step by step, never taking my eyes off her, ensuring she never took hers off me. I might take a chance and spin around, turning my back to her, but when I faced her again, there were those eyes, staring straight into mine.

When I taught her to "Drop It!" there was an unspoken command to look up at me the minute whatever "it" was hit the floor. When I taught her to "Leave It!" the strength of my gaze held her attention. And when I taught her to "Take It!" her obedience always came with a final check for permission by glancing up at me.

Any time Stella runs—down the hall, down the street, through the park—I stand in one spot, calling her back to me, and I know the minute she stops and turns and looks at me, she's halfway home.

Stella is a dog whose very soul seems to spill out through her eyes. They're large and brown, which might seem like an obvious thing to say about a dog's eyes, but when we learn how to get our dogs to "Watch Me!" in class, I see a difference between Stella and the other dogs. Bitsy carries herself like one long tube and seems completely uninterested in raising her head to look into anybody's eyes. I half expect her master to get down on the floor himself, plant his own chin on the cold white tile to lock eyes with her. Prima and Donna seem to take offense at the very idea of looking a mere human in the eye. They snuffle and sneeze at every opportunity, and while one condescends to such nonverbal communication, the other simply gets up and walks away. Blanca absolutely loves this, although she immediately assumes a chin-down, tail-up posture, prepared to launch into action the minute her master moves. Rex will watch you, all right. I swear I saw him wink.

But Stella, oh, Stella. Her eyes drink you in.

For a moment during that first class, she wouldn't look at me. Terrified and trembling, her eyes had flitted all over the store, no doubt looking for escape—or at least someplace to hide. Then, during one of our early in-class wrestling matches where she was more likely to shred me than to "Settle," there came a moment when her eyes met mine.

> *Stella is a dog whose very soul seems to spill out through her eyes.*

And stayed. Right there, in the middle of our baby-gate circle at the back of the pet store, it was like something out of a cheesy movie. Our eyes met, and everything else seemed to disappear. We held each other, drank each other in, and without a word I told her that as long as she keeps her eyes on me, we'll be just fine.

But of course, we can't keep our eyes locked every moment of every day, so it's inevitable that a problem may arise.

Just like it did the Sunday morning I found the pudding cup.

We have an understanding about the trash in our house. Anything in the big blue can in the kitchen, the one with the swinging lid, is completely off limits to Stella. She has complete respect for that Rubbermaid boundary. But, anything left in the smaller trash cans scattered throughout the house?

Well, that's pretty much fair game. We've trained ourselves not to leave anything "foodish" in those. They are to be the repositories for tissues and packages, junk mail, and old homework. The occasional candy bar wrapper and soda can are usually safe, but anything more consumable than that needs to make its way to the kitchen trash can.

This Sunday morning, as I gather up the strewn garbage after letting Stella outside, I mentally run through the previous night's scenario.

```
SETTING: Pittman kitchen at night.
Allison pulls trash out of can, ties
bag, and leaves it in the middle of
the kitchen floor.

ALLISON: (yelling) Hey, Mikey! You
need to take the trash out!

(EXIT Allison)

CUT TO: Pittman master bedroom.
Mikey watches a mixed martial arts
match on television.
```

MIKE: (yelling) Hey, Ryan! You need to take the trash out!

CUT TO: Ryan's bedroom. Ryan is in the middle of an. intense text-message "conversation."

RYAN: (yelling) Hey, Jack! You need to take the trash out!

CUT TO: Jack's bedroom. Jack plays Guitar Hero, practicing the riff on Guns 'N' Roses' "Sweet Child of Mine." He does not respond to his brother.

FADE TO BLACK AS ENTIRE FAMILY GOES TO BED.

ENTER: STELLA, STAGE RIGHT, CROSSES TO KITCHEN. SPOTLIGHT ON TRASH BAG.

The rest, as they say, is misery.

This scene makes me think of the time the apostle Paul warned the early Christians about their garbage. Oh, it was centuries before pudding cups and plastic spoons, but there were plenty of other sources of trouble. In one of his letters to the first-century church at Corinth, he offered up a reminder of Israel's past. Back in the desert, in the days of wandering, the Hebrews were surrounded by plenty of garbage—idolatry, sexual immorality, pagan revelry. They were kept from it, not by walls or vast geographic distance, but by the veneer of God's warning: "Don't do it."

For many of them, like Stella and the Hefty bag, that barrier wasn't enough. Unlike Stella, though, they weren't let off the hook. They suffered more than hearing their name spoken in a disapproving tone. Paul wrote, "God was not pleased with most of them; their bodies were scattered over the desert" (1 Corinthians 10:5). But it doesn't end there. Those who engaged in sexual immorality—twenty-three thousand of them—were killed in one day (verse 8). Those who tested the Lord were killed by snakes (verse 9). Those who grumbled were killed by the destroying angel (verse 10).

Paul had a good reason to tell these stories to the people of the church in Corinth. He wrote, "These things happened to them as examples and were written down as warnings for us" (verse 11). By "us," he meant not only himself and his fellow first-century Christians, but anybody who has access to these scriptures. You know, the ones—like me—who have their tiny white New Testament, their battered green copy of *The Way,* or the burgundy, leather-look, gold-leaf NIV with their name engraved in the lower right-hand corner—the Bible with all those meaningful verses underlined and handy notes in the margins.

It's easy for me to look at my nice, New Testament, church-saturated life and think I'm in the clear. No warnings needed, thank you. Don't see myself engaging in any pagan revelry this weekend. (Although I might want to keep one eye open over my shoulder for that destroying angel...) But in that moment, Paul reaches through the pages, grabs me by my collar, and says, "So, if you think you are standing firm, be careful that you don't fall!" (verse 12). I'm certain the original manuscript addressed me by name.

That Saturday night, Stella and I thought we were standing firm. We only had one week of Intermediate Obedience left. Stella would regularly "Leave It!" and "Drop It!" and "Sit!" on command. The days of random destruction seemed to be over. Even her personal toys were now subjected to gentler treatment. Sure, Cheeto was literally an empty shell of its former self, but Squirrel's head was still intact—setting a record of capitation.

Mike, the boys, and I had all disappeared into our rooms, turned off our lights, and closed our doors in preparation for the next day's worship. All in ignorance of the enticing, forbidden attraction for Stella in the middle of the kitchen.

I can picture the scene. The house is quiet. And dark. Maybe there's a noise outside—one of the big, barky dogs sounding the alarm for the neighborhood possum, or the neighbor's ne'er-do-well son tearing down the street in his rattletrap car, speakers blaring. Something pulls Stella from her sleep at the foot of Jack's bed, and she wanders out into the hall. The only sound is the jingle of her tags (and possibly slight snoring from behind our bedroom door). She ambles to the backdoor and presses her nose against the window. Perhaps she even nudges the tiny crack between the door and the frame in an attempt to sniff out the latest late-night news. She might sit there for a minute, wondering if any of us will hear her and get up to let her out. In fact, she probably makes a quick, trotting tour of the hallway to see if she can entice any of us out of our beds.

> *It's easy for me to look at my nice, New Testament, church-saturated life and think I'm in the clear.*

Then, back to the door. Back to the glass—peering

through the pane at the darkness outside. It's obvious no one else is getting up; she might as well go back to sleep…but not before a quick midnight snack.

She turns to walk into the kitchen. She's really only going to munch a few kernels of dog food, really. (OK—cat food…but what Clancie-the-cat doesn't know won't hurt her.) There's a thin beam of blue moonlight shining through the dining room window shades, spotlighting a large, plastic anomaly in the middle of the kitchen floor.

Stella sniffs.

Mmm…pudding/meat/tacos/chips.

And she waits to be told, "No!"

And she waits to be told, "Leave It!"

And she waits to be called away, distracted with a treat, escorted outside. But there's nothing. Just the soft sounds of a sleeping house. A clock chime. The rustle of a mattress. The rooms are dark in all directions.

She sniffs the yellow plastic ties. Nothing.

She puts a tentative paw in the pursed opening. Not a sound.

No rebuke. No reprimand.

The pudding cup—my son Charlie's late-night snack—is right at the top.

All she needs is one other set of eyes. Someone to see her and stop her.

It's too much temptation for one little dog to bear.

Paul offers these words of comfort to anybody who might be left with a bag of tempting trash in the middle of a seemingly dark and deserted kitchen: "No temptation has seized you except what is common to man. And God is faithful; he will not let you be tempted beyond what you can bear. But when you are tempted, he will also provide a way out so that you can stand up under it" (1 Corinthians 10:13).

I live in a world surrounded by every evil that enticed those Israelites in the desert with Moses. Hey, my *house* plays host to just about every Sinai-inspired vice. I have idols that vie for my attention and affection. I sometimes watch movies and television shows laced with sexual immorality, laugh at the jokes, and long—momentarily—for a taste of life in *the City.* I test my Lord, living with one foot firmly entrenched in sin, even as I grumble about the fact that my other foot doesn't seem strong enough to haul me out of it. Worse, I grumble about the fact that God allows it to exist. If I'd been back in that desert, I would have been death number 14,273.

But God doesn't need me to be an example of "What

Happens When You Disobey." In fact, He's devised a fool-proof plan for obedience, and it starts with the same step as Stella's.

"Watch Me!"

Alone in that kitchen, Stella was left with her own eyes. Had I been available to peek around the corner, glance up from my place on the couch, or call to her from the hallway to bring her to meet my gaze, she would not have fallen into disobedience. Alas, Stella is stuck with a very human, fallible master—utterly lacking in omniscience.

But my Master! What a comfort it is to serve a Master who never sleeps. "The eyes of the LORD are everywhere, keeping watch on the wicked and the good" (Proverbs 15:3). Some might see that as threatening, like God is looking down, waiting to catch us when we mess up so He can heap punishment on the wicked and have a reason to chastise the good. But they're wrong. He simply knows that as we're wandering through our lives, we're going to come across those tempting Hefty bags. We're going to find ourselves in situations we shouldn't be in, wanting to do things we know we shouldn't, and looking around, hoping to find somebody to tell us not to.

God just doesn't want us to have to look very far.

11

Clean Up, Aisle Seven

"Stay!"

O you who hear prayer,
    to you all men will come.
When we were overwhelmed by sins,
    you forgave our transgressions.
Blessed are those you choose
    and bring near to live in your courts!

PSALM 65:2–4

$\mathcal{S}$tella runs into the kitchen, called in not by my voice, but by the unmistakable sound of my opening a Ziploc baggie of cheese slices. Moments ago, she was sound asleep on her corner of the couch, but the sound of the refrigerator door must have sprung her from sleep, and the sound of the cheese baggie is nothing less than a clanging snack bell. A month ago, before our Intermediate Obedience adventure, Stella would have launched herself at me, planted her paws firmly on my legs, and scratched for my attention. But today she skids to a stop, looks up at me, and gives a lady-like lick of her lips.

At that moment, I completely forget about my youngest son, Charlie, who is in the back of the house playing a computer game and waiting for the ketchup and cheese sandwich he eats every day for lunch. Instead, I take advantage of this teachable moment and hold out my crooked, Ghost of Christmas Future pointing finger and give Stella a silent command.

She takes one more glance at the cheese and obeys, sitting nub-down on the floor.

"Good girl!" I say.

I send the orange square flying toward her, saying, "Leave it!" as it makes a cold, slapping sound when it hits the floor. Stella gazes at the cheese, but when I repeat the command, she looks right up at me. Her eyes never leave mine, even as I take one step away.

"Stay." I hold my hand up as a signal.

She doesn't move.

I walk slowly backwards until I reach the threshold between the kitchen and dining room. Stella is frozen in front of the dishwasher, the cheese flat on the floor in front of her, our eyes fixed on each other.

"Take it!" I say, giving the little hand-clap command, and she obeys with relish, scraping the cheddar treat off the floor. She's about to trot out of the kitchen when I once again give her the command to "Sit!" She obeys. I tell her to "Stay!" and take one more step into the dining room.

"Stay," I repeat, holding up my hand. Then, I take one more step backward, this time turning the corner—out of her sight. I take one, two, three quick breaths, then poke my head around the corner. She looks at me, cocking her head to one side, but doesn't stand up.

"Stay," I repeat, and disappear again, counting slowly to ten before checking back. There she is. Still.

"Good girl," I whisper and then repeat the command. This time I walk clear to the middle of the family room and wait. Nothing. Thrilled with what a good, obedient dog she's grown to be in the past few weeks, I decide to test her.

"Come here, Stella!" I call in my brightest voice, and just like that she comes tearing around the corner. Grabbing a handful of crunchy dog treats, I decide to put Stella through the ultimate test. Outside, front yard, leashless. She's set to charge out the door the minute I open it, but my simple command of "Wait" stops her in her tracks. Well, *stop* might not be the right word…more like *slows* as she assumes a nervous pacing in the entryway, which she continues until I call her out—off the front porch and into the yard.

I toss her a piece of a biscuit when she sits, then hold another bit in my hand as I encourage her "Down!" and "Down!" until she's lying flat-bellied in the crispy summer grass. I drop a treat in front of her and tell her to "Leave It!" then hold up a hand and instruct her to "Stay!" She looks up at me, raising her eyebrows at the arbitrary circumstances of these commands, but she obeys. I inch backwards all the way to the sidewalk, reinforcing my command with a constant stare. Distractions abound up and down the block. Skateboard wheels click along the sidewalk across the street. Cars roll by at a painstaking twenty miles per hour. The big, barky dogs resound from behind their fences all over the neighborhood.

But Stella doesn't move.

I take a chance and turn my back to her, stepping sideways, crab-like, toward our driveway. A quick glance over my shoulder reassures me that Stella hasn't budged, except for her head, which is turned in my direction.

"Stay," I remind her, twisting my entire body to show her the palm of my hand.

Channeling my inner Charlie's Angel, I inch my way around to the other side of our green minivan, leaving Stella essentially alone in the world, frozen in place by my command. I'm proud of her to the point of bursting. Every command perfectly mastered. There was a time when I was afraid we would have to take Stella through Remedial Obedience—a class with older, tough dogs that meets in some rundown feed supply store. But these past few moments send my heart soaring. I'm confident she'll demonstrate her behaviors perfectly on our last Saturday. Oh, there probably won't be any kind of a stage for her to walk across, but certainly there would be some kind of a diploma or certificate. If nothing else, I still have the sales receipt for the ninety-nine dollars I spent on the class. That alone would be worth framing for display on our family wall of fame.

I glance down the street and see a familiar sight about ten houses down. We call her Mrs. Walkindog. She's a very tall, elegant, elderly lady who walks her dog with relentless regularity. The dog itself—a dingy white Pomer-anian—scuttles dutifully at the end of its leash. The remarkable aspect of this neighbor-hood fixture is the big orange cat that follows respectfully—ten paces behind—everywhere they go. Stella and I encounter this entourage on occasion, and it's never a pretty sight. Mrs. Walkindog's pom takes to jumping and spitting, and Stella's hackles rise up in a bushy black triangle just above her tail-nub. There's never any lunging or baring of teeth, just an awkward unpleasantness as Mrs. Walkindog and I each tug at our dogs' leashes, grinning and silently blaming each other for the whole disagreeable scene.

I'm confident she'll demonstrate her behaviors perfectly on our last Saturday.

This, I'm sure, is too much for Stella to bear. I pop out from the far side of the van, and Stella, obviously taking my reappearance as an invitation, jumps up and runs toward me. Deep down I know that this is a spark of rebellion—I never released her from her "Stay!" Given the approaching catastrophe just seven houses away, though, I welcome her and usher her inside.

Besides, I have a child who is still waiting for his lunch.

When Stella and I strut in for our final Intermediate Obedience class, we're a far cry from what we were that first week. Stella holds her head high, and if there's any dragging involved, it's *her* dragging *me*. But I've learned to handle even that, making her sit every few steps before stepping forward again, careful to keep the leash respectably loose between us.

We head for the circle of baby gates at the back of the pet store. Our greetings are a little less forced, and Stella barely takes notice of the other dogs. Everyone is present, except for Prima and Donna, the pampered yorkies who have had very little to yap about, given our summer drought. I immediately assume one of two things to be true: either the citywide silencing of windshield wipers has convinced their owners that the little yippers were cured, or they've been sent to a more exclusive obedience class—maybe one with uniform collars that meets in an old plantation house rather than the back of a pet store.

But the rest of the gang has gathered. Bitsy sits—well, as close to sitting as she can get with that broken tail and all—

at her master's feet, dull as ever. Blanca, the now four-month-old lab, happily rolls on her back, doing her best impression of a stickless, well-bred mop. And Rex? He stands just inside the baby-gate circle, leaning a little, counting down the minutes to the final bell, then it's summer city, baby.

Stella and I walk through the gate and take our place by the fourth chair from the left. Ramon won't teach any new behaviors today. Instead, it's a last opportunity to prove ourselves as a team—confident master and obedient dog—to our instructor. After six weeks of instruction, we should all be changed beings. It's like the instruction given to the Israelites when they came to worship at the temple: "When the people of the land come before the LORD at the appointed feasts, whoever enters by the north gate to worship is to go out the south gate; and whoever enters by the south gate is to go out the north gate. No one is to return through the gate by which he entered, but each is to go out the opposite gate" (Ezekiel 46:9). True, there's just one gate here, and a plastic circle in the back of a pet store is hardly a temple, but I don't think God's directive is based solely on geography. It's the image of a journey, moving forward, not looking back—and being changed along the way.

As I look around, it seems Stella is the only one to show any real growth. Bitsy still bears that expression of aloof confusion,

Blanca is still a furry blur, and Rex appears a bit too cool for any of this. Maybe because, in all fairness, Blanca is still a puppy, Rex is a repeater essentially auditing the course, and Bitsy never had any real problems to begin with. She may have had a bro-ken tail, but Stella had come to class with a broken spirit—she and I were broken away from each other. Our time and all we've learned within these gates have healed us together.

> *After six weeks of instruction, we should all be changed beings.*

We're ready for this.

I brought the good treats today. At Ramon's instruction, I lay a little path of them along aisle seven—gerbil and ham-ster homes. Then, I lead Stella right past them, saying, "Leave it…leave it…leave it," and pausing occasionally to have my pretty girl sit nicely while store customers stop to greet her.

The final demonstration is "Stay!" For that, we all take our dogs to the back of the store, tell them to "Sit!" and then "Down!" Next, we step away, leaving them amid all the dis-tractions of a pet store—people, dogs, the distant squeak of mice—while we walk backwards down the adjoining aisle.

I have no problems getting Stella to sit. However, as soon as I try to coax her "Down!" something happens that hasn't happened in a long time. Four weeks to be exact. She looks up at me with eyes full of distrust, squats, and piddles.

"Oh, Stella," I say, making no attempt to hide my disappointment.

My older sons came with me to this class, so I immediately send one of them off to get a handful of paper towels, which are placed strategically throughout the store. Ramon is a few aisles down fawning over Bitsy, and I figure we can clean up the mess and get Stella back on track before he notices. When my son returns with the paper towels, we wipe the floor quickly and start again.

By now, though, Stella is nervous, and her attempt to make amends manifests in another tiny puddle the minute I tell her to sit.

"Stella!" I say, more harshly this time. I'm upset, not only at the repeat performance, but the fact that this time she does it right in front of Ramon.

"Maybe you need to take her outside." His tone is polite, of course, but I sense a bit of frustration in his voice too.

I know Stella too well to think that she has any real need to go outside, but I'm not about to argue with the instructor. I pick up my end of the leash and lead Stella out to the little grassy area in the parking lot placed solely for this purpose. I wait. And wait. Stella stands in place, mouth open, tongue hanging out, happy as can be. After a few minutes it's clear she's not going to go, so we head back inside. I'm hoping all she really needed was a change of scenery.

Our spot along the back wall is right in front of an impressive display of doggie beds. She looks positively tiny in comparison to the enormous plaid cushions that tower behind her. Then, like I have a thousand times before, I tell Stella to "Sit!" She complies, and I praise her, give her a treat, and command her to "Stay!" then head down the aisle.

Crisis over.

I'm halfway down the aisle when Ramon comes up and informs me that she needs to be "Down!" All the way down.

Feeling chastised myself, I trudge toward Stella, treat in hand, ready to encourage her to lie down when, to my chagrin, a pale yellow puddle emerges from underneath her.

"Stella!" Now I'm more upset than I ever have been at any of her indiscretions, and I immediately send the boys off for more paper towels.

"No," Ramon says, and my sons stop as quickly as Reese would have in similar circumstances. "The problem is, Stella doesn't want to lie down."

Obviously.

"So," Ramon continues, taking on the persona of the detective in the final act of any given *Matlock* episode, "she makes pee-pee so she doesn't have to lie down."

Now, I love this dog beyond reason, but not even I can imagine such complex reasoning coming from her pretty little head.

"Sometimes you have to *make* the dog obey. Now you," he points to me, "you go down that aisle and wait."

I obey with the acquiescence of a well-trained retriever. As I'm backing down the aisle, Ramon coaxes Stella to lie down, and the puddle beneath her widens.

"Tell her to stay!" Ramon says, and I hold up my hand to give the command. The minute I speak, Stella scrambles, trying to get to her feet. At her first jerking movement, though, Ramon's hand grasps her neck, holding her down.

"Tell her to stay!" Ramon repeats, and I try, but I'm unable to speak. I don't know why she's chosen this moment to be rebellious. I don't know what could possibly have gone wrong to make her decide to throw away everything we've achieved together. But she has. When she looks at me now, the lifeline of trust that's been constant between us for the past month is absent. Instead, she peers at me, then looks away. Her eyes alternate between panic and shame.

She's being held to the floor, covered in her own mess, and I know exactly how she feels.

Because I've been in the exact same place.

I can look back (sometimes far back, sometimes not so far) and see mess after mess I've made in my life. Financial holes I dug for myself, unhealthy relationships I refused to walk away from, stupid choices made while I was mired in rebellion. I spent years refusing to leave what God told me to "Leave!" Turning my back on what He wanted me to "Take!" Huge chunks of my life when He wanted me to "Sit!" and "Stay!" and "Settle" with Him. Instead, I chose to make my life an unfathomable mess and then roll around in it, scrambling to try to get myself out.

So, what held me down? The apostle Paul says, "For our struggle is not against flesh and blood, but against the rulers, against the authorities, against the powers of this dark world and against the spiritual forces of evil in the heavenly realms" (Ephesians 6:12).

That desperate, defeated feeling; the unmistakable sense of having messed up your life beyond repair; that slow, sinking, breathless trap—none of it is of God, but it can bring you to Him.

Now, our God, hear the prayers and petitions of your servant. For your sake, O Lord, look with favor on

your desolate sanctuary. Give ear, O God, and hear…
We do not make requests of you because we are righteous, but because of your great mercy.

O Lord, listen! O Lord, forgive! O Lord, hear and
act! For your sake, O my God, do not delay. (Daniel
9:17–19)

I imagine these words on Stella's heart, even as Ramon has
a grip on her, teaching her a lesson, when a spark of anger
builds up inside me. Yes, she's showing disobedience. And yes,
he's the instructor—a great one at that. But at this moment,
he's a flesh and blood ruler, the authority she struggles against,
and I can't stand it. An overwhelming sense of love for my
girl—a jealous love wrapped up in territorial protection—
floods my heart. She's less than ten feet away, but it seems like
we're worlds apart. In these final moments as I watch Stella
struggle to free herself from her own fear and the grip that
holds her down in the filth of her rebellion, all I want to do is
call her to me. To say, "Stella! Come here, pretty girl! Come
here, baby!"

Because maybe she didn't "Sit!"

Maybe she didn't lie "Down!"

Maybe she didn't "Stay!"

But I am her master, and she is overwhelmed by sin. I want to grant her grace, just as God granted grace to me.

At one time we too were foolish, disobedient, deceived and enslaved by all kinds of passions and pleasures. We lived in malice and envy, being hated and hating one another. But when the kindness and love of God our Savior appeared, he saved us, not because of righteous things we had done, but because of his mercy. He saved us through the washing of rebirth and renewal by the Holy Spirit, whom he poured out on us generously through Jesus Christ our Savior. (Titus 3:3–6)

"Just let her go," I say to Ramon. I'm not pleading, and I'm not terribly bossy. It's a quiet assertion, and without any discussion, Ramon takes his hand off Stella's neck, and she runs to me. She needs a bath, but I don't care. I drop to my knees to meet her and welcome her into my arms. "That's my girl," I say over and over, softly into her ear, and I get the distinct feeling that Ramon doesn't approve. Or maybe he just doesn't understand. After all, Stella hasn't earned praise. She hasn't followed the rules and precepts that would prescribe such a gracious reception.

But then, grace is a hard concept for a lot of people.

What is easier, though, is the concept of the reward—recognition for a job well done. And there's plenty of that for Stella. In spite of her lapse in the final hour of Intermediate Obedience training, or maybe to prevent us from registering for the class again, Stella graduates. We might leave through the same baby gate we entered, but we're not the same. Stella holds her head high, and I clutch a plastic bag emblazoned with the store logo. Inside is a certificate of achievement with Stella's name, a new throwing disc, a sample bag of beef-flavored treats, and a 20 percent off coupon for anything in the store. All quite valuable for the bits and pieces of the life Stella and I lead together. All very nice recognition for Stella's accomplishment. But ultimately, all unnecessary. We needed nothing more than the leash that binds us.

Today I think back to those final moments in Intermediate Obedience—to my entire history with Stella—and wonder. What if I'd waited for Stella to prove herself worthy of my love? What if I'd refused to reach out to her, to train her, until she'd given me some tangi-

What if I'd waited for Stella to prove herself worthy of my love?

ble gesture of her worthiness to be my darling? In his prayer, Daniel pleads, "O Lord, listen! O Lord, forgive! O Lord, hear and act! For your sake, O my God, do not delay" (9:19).

Why this sense of urgency? It's simple. If I'd waited for Stella to meet my expectations of the perfect dog, an ideal companion, a canine soul deserving of my affection...

I'd still be waiting.

Thankfully, I loved her first.

Author's Note

This morning, like every Friday morning, our local newscast offers two or three puppies from the city animal shelter for adoption. One of them scrambles all over the news desk; the other curls up against the anchorman's lapel. They are wonderful mixed breeds, with big eyes and big paws. During the last segment of the program, my sons watch with backpacks slung over their shoulders, ready to walk out the door. I hit Pause on the DVR before we leave so I can finish watching later when I get back home.

As I drive the boys to school, we talk about the puppies. How cute they are with their round little tummies. How much we love that sweet puppy smell. That feeling when they nuzzle against your neck.

"Not like Stella," the boys say. Stella never nuzzles. Stella smells like a porch.

I guess it's a natural thing for kids to have a constant craving for a new dog, but I play the requisite Mom card, bemoaning the idea of house training, shoe chewing, plant destroying. All those things that made our first year with Stella one of the most stressful of our lives. Of course, that was two years ago, which for kids is a lifetime. Their desire is based on the undeniable fact that puppies are cute.

When I get back home, the proof of that fact looms on the television screen as a six-week-old beaglaboxeteretreiver/shepherd mix stares into the camera. I can almost smell the milk on its breath.

Then I look over at Stella. She's draped over the arm of the couch in this odd way she has—her hind feet are on the cushion, and her head hangs over and down in a vulture-like posture. The skin on her face is hanging forward.

If the puppy on the screen is Shirley Temple, then Stella is Bea Arthur. Cute and its antithesis.

I keep the puppy frozen on the screen while I sit at the dining room table with my Cheerios and Bible. Every now and then, I glance over at Stella, who raises one perfect eyebrow at me before turning her attention back to staring at the nearly headless stuffed squirrel she's dropped on the floor beneath her. The only sound is the clink of my spoon and the rustle of pages and pen. When the last Cheerio is gone and the final prayer said, I stand up from my chair, and Stella makes a scrambling jump over the arm of the couch. She waits patiently at the kitchen corner where I'll set down my cereal bowl. She'll have the milk all slurped down by the time I've unpaused the television.

It's time for *Today*.

Before the first headline, she's curled up beside me. Licking her lips and letting out a warm, lady-like belch. I can smell the milk on her breath.

Later, when it's time to get to work, I get up, move to a different spot, and open my laptop. Stella won't budge. In fact, she might not move again until lunch. Oh, she'll rouse herself from sleep to stretch, groan, scratch, twist, yawn, and recurl herself a dozen times. Sometimes I call to her, and when she finally opens one eye I say, "Guess what, Stella bella? I'm writing a story about you!" She stretches out two long legs—claws splayed—sneezes, composes herself, then goes back to sleep.

This is how we spend our days, Stella and I. The house is silent, save for the ticking clock, the clicking keyboard, and the soft murmur of Lifetime Television. And it occurs to me—if anybody were to look in on us, they'd never believe we had such a story to tell.

Thank you for sharing it with us.

Life with Stella spans far beyond those Saturdays, and I'd love to continue sharing it with you. If you're interested in

following our ongoing story, please visit my Web site, www
.allisonpittman.com to sign up for my monthly newsletter.
Every issue includes a Dog Daze Devotional, in which Stella
continues to be a source of amusement, amazement, and ab-
solute truth.